A DREAM DERAILED

How the Left Hijacked Civil Rights to Create a Permanent Underclass

Rev. Bill Owens with Dr. Deborah Owens

ISBN 9781513652054 (softcover)

Library of Congress Control Number: Pending

Cover Design by Plaid Bison Marketing

First Printing, 2019
A New Dream Publishers
www.adreamderailed.com

A New Dream Publishers
27120 Fulshear Bend Drive
Suite 900-181
Fulshear, TX 77441

How to use the QR codes in the book
You will notice at the end of each chapter, a picture and a QR code next to it. When you scan the QR code with your phone, you will be taken to a page where you can watch the video. For iPhone users, the camera has a built-in QR code reader. To use, open your camera and hover over the QR code. Do not take a picture. When you hover over the QR Code, you will notice a URL on the screen. Touch it, and it will open the webpage where the video is located — press play to watch the video. If you have an Android phone, you'll need to download a QR code reader from the Google App store. You will then need to open the app and follow the same steps above.

Dedication

Deborah and I dedicate this book to our children David Barak and Charisma Brielle Owens. We prayed for children when we married in 1995, and they showed up in God's perfect timing on December 25, 2011 and November 3, 2012 respectively. God fulfilled His promise to us, and we are eternally grateful. The work that Deborah and I endeavor to do was sparked out of our concern for the future of our children and all children. We fight to preserve God's design for marriage, family, life, and sexuality. We want to be able to look our two innocent children in the eyes and say we have done our part to leave you a Godly legacy that you can be proud of.

To my six adult children, thirteen grandchildren, and one great-grandson, Emmanuel, I dedicate this book in hopes that each of you will do your part to reclaim the dream. Not just Martin Luther King's dream but the dream I had for each of you to be able to enjoy all the freedoms and opportunities that I couldn't enjoy just sixty shorts years ago. I dedicate this book to each of your futures and pray that you will fulfill your dreams. I want the world to know that I am proud of each of my children, and while I wasn't a perfect parent, I did everything within my power to keep the family together. Deborah and I dedicate this book with love in our hearts to God and each child, grandchild, and great-grandchild present and to come. To God be the glory!

TABLE OF CONTENTS

Chapters

ACKNOWLEDGMENTS

This book would not have been possible without the involvement of the following family, friends, and colleagues to whom we extend our heartfelt gratitude: **Dr. Ed Holliday**, who offered his time and talent with research and editing. **Ralph and Linda Schmidt**, for their words of encouragement, faithful and wise counsel, and their support throughout this endeavor. **Bishop George D. McKinney**, a trusted friend, mentor, and advisor, for providing guidance and insight. **Bill Federer**, for his dedicated work in publishing *American Minute* and for opening my eyes to President Johnson's real motives in implementing the Great Society. **Bishop Janice Hollis**, for assisting us when this book was in its infancy stage.

Also, we thank **David Nance, Ph.D.**, for transcribing some of my early notes and for providing input on the substance of this book. I want to give a special thanks to my son, **William Owens, Jr.**, for encouraging me to write this book, for his assistance with the early concepts of the book, for typesetting the book and helping us bring this project to its completion.

A heartfelt thank you to **Brian Brown** for bringing us in to work with him on the marriage issue so many years ago. It was the marriage issue that catapulted the Coalition of African American Pastors (CAAP) onto the national scene. Our work with marriage allowed us to witness first-hand the lies of the Left and prompted us to write this book. We also thank **Dr. Susan Berry and Mr. and Mrs. James Hill** for their editing and research assistance. They helped bring this book to completion!

Last but not least, I want to acknowledge my devoted and loving wife, **Dr. Deborah Owens**, for her unselfish commitment to seeing this book through to its completion. This project wouldn't have been possible without Deborah. She truly shepherded all aspects of this project, and I am eternally grateful to her!

PREFACE

When I was a student in seminary, I went through a period of deep despair over the state of my life. I was at a crossroads and had to determine, "What does God have for me to do?" I needed to hear directly from God about the path He wanted me to take to live a fulfilled life. I was living in Los Angeles at the time and knew I needed silence, solitude, and family. In December of 1988, I decided to go to Memphis to stay with my mother until January. I knew that God is a good God and wants only the best for His children. I needed and wanted God to speak to me about His plan for my life. John 14:26 says the Holy Spirit "will teach us all things and will bring to our remembrance things God has taught us." The Holy Spirit is the spirit of truth; therefore, He will lead us into the truth, not error.

Once in Memphis, I prayed with my mother, and together, we asked for direction for my life.

I did not hear God's voice immediately, however. I was in such despair that I thought my life — seemingly without a purpose — was not worth living. That Christmas Day was very hard because I realized December was ending, and my prayer to hear from God before the year was over appeared to have gone unanswered. I cried out again to God in desperation, asking Him to give me direction for my life.

Then, on my birthday, December 27, 1988, at 10:00 a.m., I received my instructions from God. Not in an audible voice, but in my spirit.

I was suddenly filled with faith, knowing that I had heard from God! His message was that I should recruit students for Oral Roberts University (ORU). I heard clear instructions in my spirit. I heard God speak recruit students for Oral Roberts University that nobody else wanted and I will give you students that everybody wants. He told me that he would give me a wife who would love me and work by my side.God said that I would go before great people. I must say that I have had the privilege of working with some of the most notable men and women in our country. God said don't touch the gold. And I thought what money? I don't' have one hundred dollars to my name. A few years later, with the Roberts' help and with the assistance of many pastors from across our nation, we were able to raise over one million dollars in scholarships for our students.

I must say that I was very excited that I heard from Heaven. I knew God was going to do something wonderful in my life! I jumped up off my knees, ran into my mother's room, and told her that God had spoken to me. She was overjoyed! I then called my lifelong friend — well-known civil rights photographer Ernest Withers — and told him what I had experienced. I also told him of my desire to go to a church that Sunday and announce that I would be recruiting students for ORU. I would assure those interested that I would get them admitted and seek the proper financing for them.

I called Elder Jasper Porter, a long-time friend, and asked him if I could come to his church Sunday and make the announcement that I recruit students for Oral Roberts University. He welcomed me and asked if I would also bring the morning sermon for him. Psalm 37:23 tells us, "The steps of a good man are ordered by the Lord," and that we can trust Him not to let us lose our way.

Asking God to speak to me and following His direction and the path He set out for me brought me from despair to a deep sense of spiritual fulfillment. I heard God's voice and obeyed. I learned to walk by faith and wisdom.

In the same way, black Americans are now in a state of despair.

Despite the successes of the civil rights movement — during which African Americans peacefully protested to obtain basic human rights — many blacks have forgotten the fact that it was their Church that was at the center of that movement, providing its moral conscience and foundation.

For as long as I can remember, the great struggle for civil rights has been empowered by the frequent use of the Bible. Its great themes of redemption, patient perseverance, and release from bondage have permeated the language we use when we discuss the civil rights movement.

There was every reason to hope the struggle for civil rights would bring about greater freedom and independence for blacks in America. Yet today, we find that many black leaders have forgotten what inspired that struggle. Many of these leaders urge black Americans to look for inspiration from government and political agendas that undermine the moral fabric of the Church — the same Church that guided the civil rights movement! Abortion, same-sex marriage, and government encroachment — which subverts religious liberty — are now all proclaimed as "freedoms" by many black leaders. To be sure, the leaders of the civil rights movement saw these as evils and evidence of sin — certainly not signs of freedom. Black Americans are at a crossroad of their own today — in many ways, even more so than before the civil rights movement. Will we turn away from a life of dependence on government and political agendas and turn back to God and His plan for us? In this book, I hope to use my life journey through segregation and Jim Crow laws along with my work as an activist in the civil rights movement and combine it with what I learned from that life-changing experience in 1988. I want my life to help blacks and Americans everywhere to reclaim the freedom and independence that God intended for us.

Let us pray that we may ask to hear God's voice and that we may direct ourselves to follow His path and guidance.

30th year
anniversary

FOREWORD

by Evangelist Alveda King
Director of Civil Rights for the Unborn

Rev. William (Bill) Owens, Sr. and his wife, Dr. Deborah Owens, are asking very serious questions. What happened in and to black America over the last half a century? Are we worse off than we were during the days of the 20th-century civil rights movement? Do most of the black community truly understand what they are voting for when they cast their vote? Can we give education a chance? Is there hope for the black family in the twenty-first century? Before you prejudge this timely treatise as just another telling and retelling of what went wrong, keep reading. Together, Bill and Deborah have a long and proven track record of identifying and then addressing problems and issues of a practical, moral, and spiritual nature; acting as change agents for a better quality of life. I've been blessed to work with both the man of God and his helpmate, the educator, for several years, during which I've witnessed first-hand their tenacity and capacity for gaining results and sowing seeds of hope and transformation where others have quit and turned away from the task at hand.

Bill and Deborah are devoted and dedicated Christian parents and grandparents who are committed to transforming our communities into safe havens for not only their family but for the families of America. Even though destruction is looming over our lives, there is hope for America. By sharing not only testimonials but case studies and best practices, Bill and Deborah have crafted a "rescue manual" for black America. In applying the principle of, "putting your mask on first," as most airlines advise passengers in case of an emergency, they are bringing a message of hope and a strategy for strengthening black America. In doing so, they cause the reader to understand that a stronger "Black America" is good for helping to bring about a "Great America."

There is an important question at the heart of this book: What happened to black America and the dream of a "Promised Land" that motivated the civil rights activists? From a personal perspective, I would answer by saying that taking prayer out of public schools and the public square happened. I would say that legal abortion happened. I would say that the redefinition of marriage happened. Many of us know what happened. Now, as we read along the paths that Bill and Deborah have tried and tested, we can ask, *"What happens next?"* without having to hang our heads and run for the nearest shelter.

Instead, we will find ourselves compelled to roll up our sleeves and join the battle that is still ahead. There have been some significant victories, most recently with the success of the forty-fifth President of the United States, who is making great progress in the areas of the economy, the sanctity of life and the safety and security of our nation. However, we cannot sit back and rely on the president and people like Bill and Deborah Owens to do all the work.

In my Christian circles, we have a saying: "Get up. Get busy doing something for the kingdom of God." That's what Rev. Bill Owens and Dr. Deborah Owens are doing. This book begins with a question about a dream derailed and ends with a challenge. I want to end with both: Will we read their book and put it away on the shelf? Or will we engage or reengage in the battle?

God bless you,

Alveda King

Evangelist Alveda King is a Christian catalyst for civil rights and spiritual victories. She is the Director of Civil Rights for the Unborn for Priests for Life, news and media contributor, an author, singer/songwriter, and producer. Her legacy as a member of the family of Rev. Dr. Martin Luther King, Jr. (daughter of civil rights activist parents Rev. A. D. and Naomi King) connects her to her 20th and 21st-century civil rights work where she has continued in service for over half a century.

1

A PROUD PEOPLE

I n the long arc of human history and oppression, there is no story more compelling than the long saga of being black in America. Black Americans have every reason to be proud people. We have known the oppression of slavery and discrimination, yet we have survived. Choose a period at any point during the past 400 years in American history: Colonial America, the early years of our fledgling republic, the Confederacy, the Jim Crow years, the pre-civil rights era, the civil rights movement, or the present day. In every era, you will see how the black experience was a vital part of shaping our nation. Moreover, you'll find an African American who helped change the course of this country. Be it Frederick Douglass, Harriet Tubman, Booker T. Washington, or Dr. Martin Luther King, Jr., the story of the black experience in the United States is a compelling one, full of pain and truth.

Fortunately, the world listens to those who thrive and can tell a story, especially a story that compels others to action. I know this story. Being black in America develops skills; only blacks can fully appreciate and deep down understand. And we can tell the story well.

The poet Maya Angelou placed her finger on the pulse of black America's heart when she wrote in "I Know Why the Caged Bird Sings":

The caged bird sings with a fearful trill
Of things unknown but longed for still And his tune is heard on the distant hill for The caged bird sings of freedom.

The history of black people in America has a universal resonance. It speaks to all people about the journey from oppression to longed-for freedom. But I must ask a question: Why is it now – after slavery was abolished over 150 years ago and after having a black president for eight years – that in black America we still hear the caged bird singing? Why?

> The history of black people in America has a universal resonance

Like the children of Israel – who were delivered by Moses out of bondage in Egypt yet wandered in the wilderness for forty years – black Americans are still searching for the Promised Land. Why are we still wandering in the wilderness? What will it take to cross the Jordan River and embrace the inheritance waiting for us?

Though black America is beyond the oppression of slavery and has already experienced the fruits of the great civil rights movement, we have yet to advance to the Promised Land of freedom and independence. We are at a crossroad and, sadly, many do not even recognize it as such. Many black Americans have been duped into believing that government "benefits" and progressive political policies that undermine religious liberty are signs of having reached the Promised Land. If you are black and live in America, do you feel like you live in the Promised Land? The answer for all black Americans, regardless of political views or economic status, is a clear and unequivocal NO!

Today, as black America still strives to attain its status as a prosperous and economically independent people, I am inspired by the leaders of the civil rights movement like Dr. King — who I believe was divinely led. He did not listen to the naysayers from either side as he embraced his mission. He stood on principles found in the Holy Bible, and as he moved mountains, he painted word pictures drawn from God's perfect wisdom.

With the vision provided by Dr. King, Rosa Parks, A Philip Randolph, Diane Nash, Bayard Rustin, Congressman John Lewis, and other civil rights leaders of the day, blacks as a people have made great strides since the Jim Crow years. Like Moses setting our people free, Dr. King helped end the great divide of segregation, and doors of opportunity opened. Our civil rights leaders demanded equal opportunities in jobs. They believed in the innate dignity of all men, which was reflected in his approach to hard work. It was Dr. King who said, "If a man is called to be a street sweeper, he should sweep streets even as Michelangelo painted, or Beethoven composed music or Shakespeare wrote poetry. He should sweep streets so well that all the hosts of heaven and earth will pause to say, 'Here lived a great street sweeper who did his job well.'" (thekingcenter.org)

Every day, I strive to meet this goal. Every night, I ask myself whether I worked honorably. It is a reminder that every action can glorify God. At the same time, it is a reminder to approach all work with humility. Our leaders reminded us that our freedom and dignity come from God, not man or government. All we need is the courage to demand our natural rights.

The men and women who sacrificed so much in America's civil rights movement forced the country to recognize the truth of Dr. King's words. Now, no one can deny that blacks are free, independent, and deserving of equal treatment. Dr. King himself is honored as one of America's great freedom-fighters. His speeches have defined our vision of equality and racial harmony.

A few decades after the March on Washington, it appeared as though the tide had turned for black America. But now, our progress seems to have stalled. Blacks in America have not yet fully embraced our hard-won freedom and independence. Despite helping to elect Barack Obama – the nation's first black president — our people are still oppressed. Worse still, that oppression has taken on an insidious form. It is an oppression that saps initiative and perpetuates the myth that black men and women need external help to succeed.

We claim to be without the power to transform ghettos that have become cesspools for crime and drugs. So many black leaders saw the election of President Obama as a milestone, but it has become a millstone. After eight years of the (supposed) political empowerment that accompanied the Obama years, we are anchored in a morass of despair. We were promised "hope," but that promise turned out to be empty political rhetoric.

Back in the real world, where African Americans are trying to build families and communities, things grew more desperate. In Chicago, every weekend brings more stories about murders and shootings. What does it say when the city of the first black president starts resembling a war zone? Like the Promised Land, the "hope and change" we were told about have become ever more elusive since the first inauguration of President Obama.

If the future were brighter, we might be able to overlook some of these problems. However, if the plight of our children is any measure, the future is equally dark.

Our children are stagnating or, worse yet, falling further behind in our inner-city schools — despite hundreds of billions of dollars spent on one progressive education reform after another. The Common Core Standards initiative, for example, was the latest progressive panacea that was supposed to shrink the "achievement gap" between black and Hispanic children and their white or Asian peers. Instead, black students are scoring worse than ever on standardized tests compared to students from other nations. So many of our children are failing to graduate and are dropping out of schools. Why?

How can we be surprised by the lackluster numbers when we can't even guarantee our children a safe place to learn? Too many of the school's black children attend are unsafe environments, where learning is next to impossible due to an atmosphere of chaos and danger.

Unable to solve the crisis, progressive policies pretended it didn't exist by redefining what it means to be disruptive. During Barack Obama's administration, inner-city schools were forced to stop reporting some behavioral problems demonstrated by black and Hispanic children. The "ivory tower" theory behind this move was that they were acting in the name of social justice. What they ignored is the fact that these policies hurt other minority students. Ignoring bad behavior punishes the other students in that school, who are often minorities as well. (See Appendix B, Education.)

So, what is the result of this social justice attempt to redefine deviancy? Children are learning they can get away with threatening behavior and assault — schools where no one can learn. Teachers have been driven away from the profession. The only people who benefited from this policy were politicians, interest groups, and the consultants who were no doubt ready with another magic fix for education.

Shouldn't our black children — like all children — learn there are limits and boundaries and that such behavior has consequences? And shouldn't our black children — like all children — be able to learn in classrooms and schools that are not constantly disrupted by the belligerent and threatening behavior of other students, be they black, brown, or white? If black children are treated differently than white children, is that not another form of government tyranny?

But children aren't the only ones being smothered by the good intentions of too much government. Black businessmen and women also know what it means to see their efforts frustrated by intrusive policies. Barriers to entrepreneurship and the chokehold of excessive regulation have left us feeling helpless as we've tried to build our businesses. How can we fully embrace our independence and unleash our creativity when we are still enslaved by government rules that block us from running our businesses as we know best?

This is the conundrum: we are a proud, post-slavery, post-Jim Crow, post-civil rights people. Yet we are still enslaved and dependent. Why?

Well, let's consider for a moment that we, as a people, are still voting over 90 percent for one political party. In election after election, we place Democrats in positions of power, from mayors of our large cities to governors and even the presidency. Yet, black people are still hurting, still dying. Who is listening? Too many black politicians have made a career out of blaming those in power, but they never look in the mirror to see that they've become who they railed against. As the career politicians have become wrinkled and old, the people they represent are often worse off than when they were first elected. Does that make sense?

I have lived to see a black man win the White House and get re-elected. President Barack Obama started with a filibuster-proof, Democrat-led United States Senate and a powerful, progressive House of Representatives. It was socialism on steroids, and more political power than Dr. King could have ever hoped for in his wildest dreams. What happened?

No, really, think about it. The Republicans could not stop any legislation because the Democrats had a filibuster-proof U.S. Senate. Any legislation that black America wanted was within reach.

So, what did black America get for helping to concentrate unprecedented power in the hands of the Democratic Party? Again, I say, look around. Are our inner cities with their Democratic mayors better off for helping to put President Obama into the Oval Office for eight years? With all the political power the Democratic Party mustered by garnering over 90% of the black vote, you would think black America could see a huge difference in black communities. What do we see? The only big gains experienced by black Americans under the Obama administration are in death and sorrow. If an expectant mother has a black baby in her womb, she has more taxpayer-funded Planned Parenthood clinics in her neighborhood that allow her to murder that baby if she chooses, and an astounding number of black mothers do. So sad.

America today bears a disturbing resemblance to the famous opening line from Charles Dickens' *A Tale of Two Cities*: "It was the best of times; it was the worst of times."

Just as Dickens noted when he wrote about the French Revolution, there is now a kindred spirit awakening black men and women who are wondering what has gone wrong. For eight years, we had a black president. But we as a people are worse off now than we were before he started!

> The only big gains experienced by black Americans under the Obama administration are in death and sorrow

In 2008, when black America cheered all election night long, who would have believed that eight years later, we would be asking what happened to the "hope and change?"

With Obama as president, LGBT activists were able to enact same-sex marriage throughout the land by claiming that marriage between two people of the same sex was the "civil rights issue of our time!" Our country's borders were open, and illegal immigrant children without parents were encouraged to cross our border, provided with lawyers, and placed in communities across the country. President Donald Trump complains today about the loopholes in our immigration laws called "catch and release." By law, an illegal immigrant that crosses the border must be allowed to stay until a court date is set. Most never make it to court. They stay in the United States illegally. The Democratic Party has used its political power to help illegal immigrants more than they help black America!

With Obama as president, Wall Street executives and stockholders made out handsomely, but what about black people as a whole? Yes, some blacks have become very successful, but in our cities, fear rules the streets. Black on black murders in city after city are like statistics from war zones. When I go into a hospital, I look for black doctors. What I regularly see, however, are doctors from India, Pakistan, Egypt, Vietnam, Russia, and Cuba. I am left wondering, "Where are the black doctors?" I have met only two black doctors in Henderson where I live, and they were both from Africa. I know we have some black doctors in our country, but I haven't met them. We have been in America for 400 years, and it appears to me that foreigners hold more medical positions than American born blacks.

And it's not just the medical positions. Where are the black entrepreneurs?

Under a black president, we saw unchecked illegal immigration — even as research groups warned that this would be devastating to black unemployment. But the Democratic Party had grown complacent about black votes and craved a new demographic to secure their power. They shifted to a stance that embraced almost no barriers to illegal immigration, regardless of the effect on the black family. We'd served their purpose by putting them into power, and now we were expected to embrace policies that put us out of work. It wasn't until after President Trump took office that black unemployment began to rebound, yet he has been called racist for wanting to enforce immigration laws that would protect black jobs. This attempt to manipulate black voters again is disheartening — especially when total Democratic rule turned America into the land of opportunity for everyone but a few black Americans.

After 400 years in America, 150 years after the Civil War and the destruction of slavery, 60 years after the great civil rights movement blacks haven't reached the Promised Land. Please come with me as I put you on the tip of a needle and use my memories to weave together where we are and why we, as a people, have not yet reached the

Promised Land. Permanent scars are seared into the consciousness of black America, and — no matter how long I live — I will never be able to forget. But as I am a student of what has been, I also know what can be. Come and follow me. There is a path to the Promised Land.

A Poem by
William
Owens, Jr.
We Are A
Resilient
People

2

THE FOUNDERS' SEEDS OF FREEDOM BRING FORTH FRUIT

F reedom for black Americans did not come all at once. But the seeds for it were planted when our nation was born. Most Americans associate the end of slavery with the Civil War, but Abraham Lincoln had a dream of freedom that was rooted deep in America's Declaration of Independence. Former President-turned-Congressman John Quincy Adams taught the newly elected Congressman Lincoln of Illinois his plan to free the slaves. Lincoln was a pallbearer at Adams' funeral and, years later, pressed forward with Adams' dream of freeing all slaves.

John Quincy Adams inherited this dream from his father, John Adams, who was on the committee to write the Declaration of Independence in the Second Continental Congress. So, when Dr. King spoke of his dream for America in front of the Lincoln Memorial, it was the continuation of the Founders' dream that "All men are created equal and endowed by their Creator with certain unalienable rights."

In fact, as Dr. King was delivering his famous "Dream" speech in front of the Lincoln Memorial, not far away was the Jefferson Memorial with art depicting the committee writing the Declaration of Independence. And now today — between the Lincoln Memorial and the Jefferson Memorial — stands the Martin Luther King, Jr. Memorial. I am proud that our nation has created a memorial to a Baptist minister, a civil rights icon, and one of the greatest citizens that America has ever produced.

In his "I Have a Dream" speech, Dr. King declared, "When the architects of our republic wrote the magnificent words of the Constitution and the Declaration of Independence, they were signing a promissory note to which every American was to fall heir." [1]

Dr. King often spoke of the greatness and genius of our Founders. In his famous "Letter from Birmingham Jail"[2] he wrote:

"One day the South will know that when these disinherited children of God sat down at lunch counters, they were in reality standing up for what is best in the American dream and for the most sacred values in our Judeo-Christian heritage, thereby bringing our nation back to those great wells of democracy which were dug deep by the founding fathers in their formulation of the Constitution and the Declaration of Independence."

I believe that one day, all America will know that the 21st Century black conservative pioneers, when swimming upstream against the mainstream media and leftist ideology, were once again lifting, "the most sacred values in our Judeo-Christian heritage." Like our Founding Fathers, Lincoln, and Dr. King, they helped transform all our experiences into the necessary ingredients needed to finally cross the Jordan River into the Promised Land.

Three Founding Fathers who all served on the committee to write the Declaration of Independence – Benjamin Franklin, Thomas Jefferson, and John Adams – have been assaulted in a relentless attack of political correctness by leftist ideologues. These progressives attack our Founding Fathers as slave-holding white males who set up a system of laws to build and protect white male supremacy. But to buy into that argument dismisses the geniuses who conceived the principles of liberty that allowed free people to govern themselves. It was a kind of freedom unique to anything else on the entire planet at that time in history, and it would become the blueprint for our modern conception of individual liberty. These patriots did more than just put together a nation ruled by laws. They cultivated the roots of modern democratic governance and crafted a philosophy that would make the United States of America the greatest nation ever.

At the time, the world was amazed that this upstart nation could thrive without the help of kings and overlords. Indeed, we did more than just thrive. We spread our ideals and saw them take root elsewhere. The Founders' idea of democracy blossomed on the face of the earth.

For many, the contrast between the ideals of freedom in America's founding documents and the reality of our slave-holding past is too painful, almost hypocritical. However, there is another way to look at this contradiction. By basing the nation in ideals of freedom and liberty, which exist through the will of God, the Founders guaranteed a reckoning at some point in the fledgling country's future. The two contrary ideas could not be balanced indefinitely — one day, America would have to face the fact that slavery is antithetical to everything we stand for.

> Though the future of freedom for the enslaved was delayed, the seeds of justice were planted

Though the future of freedom for the enslaved was delayed, the seeds of justice were planted. The writings of Franklin, John Adams, and Jefferson leave no doubt that they would have preferred freedom for slaves during the founding of America. But these men had to rest on the faith that freedom for the slaves would come through another generation. It was a bridge too far in 1776, but, by faith, they believed in liberty and in the will of the American people to do the right thing in the next generation.

Thomas Jefferson, who penned the immortal words that would underline the hypocrisy of slavery in a free society: "All men are created equal," wasn't just engaging in rhetoric. Before he entered politics, Jefferson worked as a lawyer. While he specialized in land cases, Jefferson also took cases where he tried to free slaves, including *Howell v. Netherland* (1770), where he fought to free a mixed-race man who he believed had been illegally enslaved.

Benjamin Franklin, who at one time believed the myths of racial inferiority perpetuated in the 18th century, eventually found truth and enlightenment. In 1763, he wrote a letter to an English friend in which he stated, "I was overall much pleased, and from what I then saw, have conceived a higher opinion of the natural capacities of the black race than I had ever before entertained. Their apprehension seems as quick, their memory as strong, and their docility in every respect equal to that of white children."[3]

In 1787, Franklin became President of the Philadelphia Society for the Relief of Free Negroes Unlawfully Held in Bondage, also known as the Abolition Society.[4]

Finally, in a 1790 letter written shortly before Franklin's death to then-Vice President John Adams, Franklin wrote in favor of ending the slave trade in America:[5]

Sir,

At the request of the Pennsylvania Society for the Abolition of

Slavery,

I have the Honour of presenting to your Excellency the enclosed Petition

which I beg leave to recommend to your favourable Notice. Some further particulars respecting it, requested by the Society will appear in their letter to me, of which I enclose a Copy, and have the Honor to be

Sir, Your Excellency's most obedient & most humble Servant

B Franklin

Presid[ent] of the Society

His Excell[enc]y John Adams Esq

Vice President of the United States

Although we lack the historical perspective to understand that era, we can recognize the lies behind modern attempts by progressives to denigrate our Founding Fathers by rewriting history in their distorted ideology. The truth is seen in the freedom and prosperity we enjoy, especially when compared to the conditions of oppression or poverty that many citizens of the world experience.

Rather than despair over the flaws of our Founders, we should recognize how they provided a model for pursuing freedom that is still valid today. We can discover the seeds they planted, study how these seeds have been cultivated, and in some cases, pull the weeds and re-discover a garden full of freedom plants that have been neglected.

> Progressives seem focused on cultivating hate and fear

Progressives seem focused on cultivating hate and fear. However, their culture of outrage cannot withstand a grateful heart and a sense of perspective. An attitude of gratitude provides a sense of confidence that is resistant to lies and deception. Therefore, we rarely see any leftists celebrating the genius of our Founders.

Thankfulness is taught in the Bible. Thankfulness used to be taught in our public schools, but it is systematically rooted out. How? Thanksgiving used to be celebrated by thanking God. When was the last time you heard thankfulness to God celebrated in a public school? Progressives and leftists want to eliminate any form of thankfulness to God because it is difficult to be thankful and entertain a spirit of fear and destruction.

Instead of destroying the memories and distorting the truth of our Founders, we should look for those seeds of liberty that can be cultivated. The seeds that can encourage us to muster the strength to cross the Jordan River. There is no better example of one generation passing on the fight of freedom for the enslaved than John Quincy Adams.

The son of the second president of the United States, John Quincy Adams also became president. But what many people don't know is that after his presidency, John Quincy Adams returned to the U.S. House of Representatives, where he furiously worked to end slavery in America.

History notes that while he never saw slavery abolished, Adams fought the fight with a determination that inspires us to persevere in doing what is right and just.

John Quincy Adams was described in Bill Federer's *American Minute* as a tireless champion of freedom:[6]

- Nicknamed "The Hell-Hound of Slavery" for relentlessly speaking out against slavery, John Quincy Adams singlehandedly led the fight to lift the Gag Rule which prohibited discussion of slavery on the House floor.

- In 1841, John Quincy Adams, with the help of Francis Scott Key, defended 53 Africans accused of mutiny aboard the slave ship Amistad. He argued their case before the U.S. Supreme Court and won, giving them back their freedom.

- In their defense, John Quincy Adams quoted the ideals of America's founding, stating, "The moment you come to the Declaration of Independence, that every man has a right to life and liberty, an inalienable right, this case is decided. I ask nothing more in behalf of these unfortunate men than this Declaration."

- John Quincy Adams is the only major figure in American history who knew both the Founding Fathers and Abraham Lincoln.

- Lincoln, as a freshman Congressman from Illinois, was a pallbearer at John Quincy Adams' funeral.

As noted, John Quincy Adams led a relentless fight against the institution of slavery in the U.S. House of Representatives until he died ... and even to the moment of his passing. He had a stroke on the House floor and was lifted and carried to a couch in the U.S. Capitol where he died two days later. Many in the slave-holding states hoped that the death of this "Hell-Hound of Slavery" would end the fight against slavery, but a young congressman from Illinois named Abraham Lincoln was a pallbearer at Adams' funeral. The future President of the United States was not only inspired by Adams' fight for freedom for all Americans but also spent time with the former president and listened to his plan to end slavery. The seeds to free the slaves— seeds planted by our Founding Fathers — endured.

During the Civil War, Lincoln showed bold leadership in using a rebellion and a shaken nation to free an enslaved people. It is no easy thing to shepherd a young nation through a crisis that threatens the very foundations of government. During his presidency, Lincoln probably thought he was riding a wild bull at times, but he pressed on toward the prize. We cannot know the despair he felt when he saw the lists of soldiers killed in battle. So much pain and death in the service of guaranteeing that our nation would live and freedom endure. The gut-wrenching decisions he was forced to make as Commander-in-Chief during a civil war had to be sobering and surreal.

What kept Lincoln going? The seeds of freedom planted in the Declaration of Independence and his responsibility to see slavery ended and America reborn. Lincoln knew John Quincy Adams. John Quincy Adams knew the Founders. And our Founders knew that our rights come from God Almighty! Abraham Lincoln was determined to keep America whole and to make sure slaves everywhere, "are, and henceforward shall be free."

The iron determination of Lincoln and the newly formed Republican Party would be echoed nearly a century later when Dr. King used an army of nonviolent protesters to energize a nation to get its head out of the sand and stand — stand for liberty and justice for all!

The knowledge that many of our Founding Fathers wanted freedom for the slaves and that the fight was passed on to succeeding generations inspires me. Although I am now in the later season of my life, I believe, as Lincoln did, that this nation, "under God," is now ready for a "rebirth of freedom!"

America has been blessed. We are the strongest nation the world has ever known. We have weapons that can neutralize any enemy on earth. We have an economy that is second to no other nation. With President Trump, for the first time in most Americans lives, we have more jobs available than we have workers looking for jobs. Black unemployment is now the lowest in recorded history.

And yet too many of us are still looking for answers and empowerment in the wrong places. The Trump economy is roaring as I write this book, but we are still suffering. Many in black America are addicted to government programs. And, yes, even though we have suffered and persevered through slavery, the Civil War, Reconstruction, Jim Crow laws, segregation, and the civil rights movement, we must still ask the question, "Now what?"

I am inspired that John Quincy Adams never gave up in his fight against slavery. I am inspired that he taught the young Abraham Lincoln his dream to destroy slavery. I am glad that these freedom lovers believed and could dream about an America without slavery! And, just as these former presidents had a vision for freedom, so do I.

I believe that one day, those in our inner cities will live their lives worthy of the Ten Commandments and that freed citizens will vote for candidates regardless of party affiliation — for candidates that uphold Judeo-Christian values! My prayer for now and in the future is that God will remove politicians in positions of authority who mock His name and ridicule Biblical values. And I pray that God will place into positions of authority men and women who fear the Lord and seek to serve God!

The poverty-stricken strongholds that have suffered under the heavy-handed tactics of the Democratic Party's overlords for over 50 years will soon see a new birth of freedom. I believe that. And I believe that black America will come full circle politically. The Party of Lincoln carved out the path to end slavery. The Republican Party made a home for black Americans.

I believe that new technology and ideas in education will become a transformational method to destroy poverty like General Grant destroyed the Confederate Army. The Democratic Party now stands like Richmond, Virginia did in 1865 -- surrounded by the forces of freedom. The charade cannot go on forever. Too many black Americans have seen so little progress in the past 50 years that we are ready for a big change — a huge change! We want financial independence, and the Democratic Party wants us to stay dependent on government handouts. Recently, Nancy Pelosi, Democrat Speaker of the House, called the $1,000 bonuses handed out by employers because of the 2018 Republican tax cut, "crumbs." A $1,000 bonus based on your hard work is not a crumb, and the Democratic Party didn't make it happen.

I have seen so much in my life. I remember using water fountains with signs that read "for whites only." I remember when public restrooms had signs too. I remember dreading having to drive through places like Mississippi for a funeral. It was dangerous for Blacks to be there after dark back then.

So much has been written on my inner soul that, like most people with black skin, I have an innate ability to detect when I am purposely being mistreated. And I have been mistreated.

I had so much hope in Dr. King's leadership; the entire black community suffered an unspeakable pain when he was assassinated. We have never recovered. What does God want? What prayers have yet to be answered? The Lord knows that we have prayed. Like Moses leading the children of Israel out of the Kingdom of Egypt, King and others led us out of Jim Crow and segregation. But where is Joshua? Why are we still wandering 50 years later? Do you know the way to the Promised Land?

Dr. King's dream was the rebirth of freedom that Lincoln spoke of in the Gettysburg Address. The freedom kindled in the hearts of the patriots who fought the American Revolution is the very freedom that I taste today. Yet, I fear this patriotic zeal for freedom has somehow been diminished in black America today. Gratitude and patriotism are scorned by pushers of the leftist agendas who preach hatred and resentment. Seeds of distortion to cloud our shared history will lead to bitter weeds growing in our communities. This poisonous fruit will sour all that we attempt to do for good.

Let me be clear: I seek the same freedom for myself and my family that the early patriots sought. I stand on the shoulders of patriots – black and white, red and yellow — when I declare that we, as a people, will soon get to the Promised Land.

When I grieve about where black America is today, I must be true and say what is in my heart. It pains me to hear some institutions teach that the Founding Fathers were rich, white slave owners putting together a system of government for the rich and white and powerful. This is a dangerous lie that casts historical slanders to push a political agenda! This is so wrong!

Those who rail against our Founders, whether purposefully or intentionally forget the struggles of patriots like the father and son Adams. Why would people from all over the world try to get into America unless they believe a better life is waiting for them and their children in the United States?

Black America has often been targeted by those who want to use us and exploit us. These charlatans try to persuade us to complain and find excuses for not achieving. Booker T. Washington warned African Americans about the people who make a business of, "advertising," the wrongs done to the black community, "partly because they want sympathy and partly because it pays."

Washington, one of the great figures of African American history, was writing in 1911, but his words still feel relevant. In his book *My Larger Education*, Washington warned:

"There is a certain class of race problem solvers who do not want the patient to get well because as long as the disease holds out, they have not only an easy means of making a living but also an easy medium through which to make themselves prominent before the public."

Dr. King often spoke of the deep wells of wisdom that founded this nation. Where else on this planet is there more freedom and opportunity to reach our God-given potential than here in the United States?

I am thankful for our Founding Fathers. Yes, I wish that John Adams and Benjamin Franklin could have convinced the South to end slavery – but they didn't. I wish that I could change a lot in history, but it is what it is. We cannot change the past, but with God's help, we as a people can cross the Jordan River into the Promised Land.

We must recognize that our Founding Fathers provided a Constitution in which we have seen King's dream – where little white boys and black boys can play and live together. We want the Promised Land, where economic independence for black America is prominent. It won't happen, however, without an attitude of gratitude for those who risked everything to found a nation based upon a Constitution where we are governed by laws and not men.

We live on fertile ground. Blood has been shed for our freedom in every century that black people have lived on this land. We have more opportunity than ever before --- right here and right now in America.

So, if you're asking, "Which way to the Promised Land?" I'll answer: "The way is clear."

What I am trying to show you is that it's not a new way. It has already been paved for us. The Founders of our great country began carving out the path. President Lincoln helped pave the way for us, as did Dr. King and the great civil rights leaders. All these great leaders are still with us on this spiritual journey. Their message hasn't changed.

Unfortunately, black America has changed. Many of us have become distracted and strayed from God's way for us. Many have allowed themselves to be dazzled by the promises of progressive politicians and community organizers – promises of unending government provisions. Why take the initiative in my work when the government sends me a check or a debit card to buy necessities? Why get involved in my children's education when they can have breakfast, lunch, and an afternoon snack at school, my only responsibility being to pick them up when it's time for dinner? Why go to church on Sunday and become involved in my faith community when that's the only day I have to myself?

I have a question for you. When you combine the lives and actions of the Founding Fathers, Abraham Lincoln, Dr. Martin Luther King, Jr., and other prominent leaders of that time, what do you get? You get boldness inspired to ring a liberty bell where the sound of freedom had never been heard. You get sacrifice for the greater good. You get leaders willing to walk where no one had ever walked before. You get Biblical principles practiced when odds seemed overwhelmingly difficult. Such footprints of the past can sometimes make us feel insignificant, but the Apostle Paul wrote that in my weakness, I must depend on God to make me strong. So, do we.

Rev. Owens Honored by the Tennessee Legislature

3

THE POLITICS OF WHAT WENT WRONG WITH BLACK AMERICA

N one of us can take that first step across the Jordan River until we come to terms with what has gone wrong with black America and the consequences of taking that wrong path. The adage that those who don't know history are doomed to repeat it applies to black America today. It's as if truth has been hidden. A cover-up has been instigated by those who fear what is real and seek to exploit blacks. Therefore, clouds of distortion are created by the leftists to hide the truth. They do this through media, political power, intimidation, and overt influence.

The fact is that relatively few of us are embracing the message of freedom – the message we heard from our nation's leaders.

Let's examine the following, as Bill Federer of American Minute. com has organized for us:[7]

Abraham Lincoln was a Republican.

Republicans drove the effort to adopt the 13th Amendment to the Constitution – which abolished slavery – after the Civil War.

Angry Democrats from the South who wanted slavery to continue, however, passed "Jim Crow" laws and "Black Codes" that allowed former slaves – now called "apprentices" – to be punished by their "employers" if they left their positions. These same Southern Democrats attempted to keep blacks from voting. Discrimination was alive and well!

In 1866, Republicans passed the Civil Rights Act — making freed slaves citizens of the United States — and then pushed the adoption of the 14th Amendment to ensure all former slaves were granted the rights of citizens. Not a single Democrat voted to adopt the amendment.

In 1870, with 97 percent of Democrats opposed, Republicans pushed for the adoption of the 15th Amendment that gave the right to vote to all men, regardless of their race.

Outraged that slavery had been overturned and former slaves now had the right to vote, Southern Democrats engaged in threatening activities — even lynchings — that served to frighten and intimidate freed slaves. Homegrown terrorism spread throughout the American South as state governments instituted discrimination purposely and with designed prejudice.

These events led Republican President Ulysses. S. Grant to sign into law the Enforcement Act of 1870, to ensure that anyone who attempted to deprive Americans, including freed slaves, of their civil rights, were penalized. This law was followed by the creation of the U.S. Department of Justice. Initially, the Justice Department was vigorous in its prosecution of members of the Ku Klux Klan.

Recently Dinesh D'Souza, an Indian American political commentator, filmmaker, and author, said that nowhere in America's past has there ever been recorded a Republican whoever owned slaves. He said that he was once challenged that President Grant had owned a slave through family ties. But D'Souza noted that at the time Grant owned the slave, he was a Democrat. Only later, after slavery, was ended, did he become a Republican.

A separate measure, the Ku Klux Klan Act, was enacted in 1871 by the Republican Congress to prohibit Democrat-founded groups that threatened black Americans. When violence against blacks persisted, President Grant sent troops to fight against it.

Republicans continued to work for the civil rights of black Americans, and black Americans, in turn, voted for the GOP. Many African Americans voted for Republican President Dwight Eisenhower, both in 1952 and 1956. It was during Eisenhower's administration, in 1954, that the U.S. Supreme Court decided Brown v. Board of Education, which outlawed segregated schools for black and white children.

Democrats in the South — including Robert Byrd, a former KKK member, and Gov. George Wallace — continued to oppose the civil rights of blacks and desegregation. To ensure the safety of black children, President Eisenhower ordered soldiers to escort them to school. When the president proposed legislation that would again enforce the voting rights of African Americans, Southern Democrats filibustered the measures and attempted to weaken them.

For 100 years following the Civil War, Republicans continually fought for the civil rights of black Americans as Democrats from the South opposed all attempts of equality.

The Civil Rights Act of 1964 brought about monumental change in the United States. Finally, black Americans could have complete equality. Surely, we had finally crossed the Jordan and reached the Promised Land. Blacks and whites could now eat together in public restaurants and stay at the same hotel. Discrimination in public places would finally be outlawed.

Despite having the longest filibuster in the history of the U.S. Senate, the Civil Rights Act finally passed in July 1964. What many black Americans today don't realize is that a greater proportion of Republicans voted for the Civil Rights Act than Democrats. In fact, Republican Senate Minority Leader Everett Dirksen of Illinois helped to write the civil rights legislation and led the effort to end the filibuster against it. Democrat Senators Richard Russell of Georgia and Strom Thurmond of South Carolina, however, fought to continue the filibuster.

In the U.S. House, only 63 percent of the 244 Democrats who voted on the bill approved it, while 80 percent of the 171 Republicans voted in favor of it.[8] In the Senate, the final tally was 73 in favor and 23 against the Act. Of the 67 Democrats, 69 percent approved it, while 27 of the 33 Republicans, or 82 percent, voted in favor of the Civil Rights Act.[9]

Since President Lyndon Johnson, a Democrat, signed the Civil Rights Act into law, Democratic politicians often enjoy taking credit for the Act. However, according to Ronald Kessler, author of *Inside the White House*, Johnson explained his efforts to persuade his party's leaders to support a watered-down version of the original bill with a very revealing statement.

"I'll have those niggers voting Democratic for the next 200 years," Johnson reportedly said.[10]

In my view, Johnson was a racist. He reportedly referred to the Civil Rights Act as "the nigger bill." Johnson biographers Robert Caro[11] and Robert Dallek confirm the president's prejudice against blacks.

MSNBC[12] reports on Caro's depiction of Johnson, especially the president's unrepentant racism:

"According to Caro, Robert Parker, Johnson's sometime chauffer, described in his memoir, *Capitol Hill in Black and White*,[13] a moment when Johnson asked Parker whether he'd prefer to be referred to by his name rather than 'boy,' 'nigger,' or 'chief.' When Parker said he would, Johnson grew angry and said, 'As long as you are black, and you're gonna be black till the day you die, no one's gonna call you by your goddamn name. So, no matter what you are called, nigger, you just let it roll off your back like water, and you'll make it. Just pretend you're a goddamn piece of furniture.'"

Dallek[14] observed the same quality in Johnson, as MSNBC reports:

"In Flawed Giant, Johnson biographer Robert Dallek writes that Johnson explained his decision to nominate Thurgood Marshall to the Supreme Court rather than a less famous black judge by saying, 'When I appoint a nigger to the bench, I want everybody to know he's a nigger.'"

Despite Johnson's racist views, I will credit him for signing the Voting Rights Act of 1965. The Act was critical in that it sought to overcome legal barriers at the state and local levels that blocked blacks from exercising their right to vote as was provided for under the 15th Amendment to the U.S. Constitution.

Why do I discuss how the Civil Rights Act came about and the prejudice of Lyndon Johnson? Because — as I noted earlier — we, as a people, are still voting over 90 percent for the Democratic Party when history demonstrates that throughout our people's struggle to attain equality, Democrats were largely fighting against us!

Today, I am often embarrassed by many of those who profess to be leaders for black Americans. They stand on the shoulders of giants but spread ignorance about black history. In part because of them, too many people don't know what happened in the long struggle for civil rights that started as soon as slavery was abolished in America.

Consider, for example, Black Lives Matter, an organization that claims to be for racial justice. I marched with Dr. King during the real civil rights movement – which was a peaceful demonstration, and I can tell you that Black Lives Matter leaders bear no resemblance to the great civil rights leaders. They are little more than a radical and uninformed group who have courted the media while enticing black youth into a false reality. They teach a distorted view of history, and they don't come close to utilizing the ten commandments that Dr. Martin Luther King, Jr. espoused in his non-violent march for civil rights.

Black Lives Matter isn't just misguided; it is actively hurting our cause. The group isn't about lifting people; it is about grabbing headlines, spreading outrage, and courting the worst elements of the Left. Black Lives Matter is inflaming black communities and endangering our young people. Inciting violence and dabbling in its own racist tendencies, this group embraces a leftist agenda that wants to destroy America and rebuild it like dedicated Marxists. With no sense of irony, they frequently call others fascists, then drown out opposing voices with fascism all their own. America was born with freedom of speech. Groups like Black Lives Matter who seek to deny freedom of speech to those they disagree with are propagating a new form of fascism in our country.

I don't see anything positive in this movement to help our youth. And, sadly, this group is setting our young people up to fail. They are misleading them and misinterpreting Scriptures to support their twisted agenda. They have joined with far-left activists who demand we renounce our faith to support same-sex marriage and abortion.

Where are the activists who understand the values at the heart of the black community? Blacks need partners who will stand with us as we stand against all evil — whether it's same-sex marriage, corrupt politicians, racism, abortion, or any of the ills that we face as Americans. The Judeo-Christian values on which this nation was founded are the rock on which black America should agree to stand. These values represent our common ground. They are woven into the fabric of our country and are dear to all Americans. I call on all pastors and ministers to reclaim what will bind us together and move us forward. "On Christ the Solid Rock I stand, all other ground is sinking sand."

> Where are the activists who understand the values at the heart of the black community?

If you don't understand my opposition to Black Lives Matter, I ask you to think again about the great civil rights marchers and then contrast them with the actions of Black Lives Matter. You can judge us by both our goals and our actions. Either way, the contrast speaks volumes. What are the Black Lives Matter protests about – what are they protesting? They have shut down highways and interrupted rallies like thugs. They are loud, angry, and rude – completely the opposite of the followers of Dr. King. We achieved our goals through peaceful demonstration, as our leaders taught us. But if young black people today follow Black Lives Matter, they will not be taught about healing America. They will be taught how to be more divisive and will risk being killed or going to prison. Dr. King's non-violent protests were successful. We won the civil rights movement just as Moses led the children of Israel out of bondage in Egypt.

We must be aware that there is something Machiavellian about the tactics of groups like Black Lives Matter. People who care deeply about racial equality are being manipulated by a far-left group that isn't honest about its agenda. And they are being manipulated to embrace violent tactics that legitimize a government decision to "seize" rights from citizens to "restore order." During the Cold War, Vladimir Lenin and the Soviets had a term for people who could be manipulated into destroying their own freedoms: "useful idiots."

Blacks should not back down nor allow themselves to be used by any group — political or not, Republican or Democrat — to further an agenda that does not align with the Word of God.

Because if we use His Word as our guiding light, we cannot be led astray. We will continue to stand for what is right and just. We stand for truth, period! I say, "All lives matter to God! All lives matter to me. All lives should matter to each of us."

But Black Lives Matter isn't the only group that has done wrong by black Americans. Let's also consider the Congressional Black Caucus (CBC) — a group that claims to be representing blacks in Congress. In January 2018, members of the CBC acted like immature children at President Donald Trump's State of the Union address. As someone who is a black father, teacher, civil rights activist, and spiritual leader, I found their behavior to be a disgrace! While the president spoke, CBC members sat in their seats, sulking. They texted on their phones and pretended to be bored. That is nothing less than childish behavior!

Once again, I say to judge them by their actions and values. What does the CBC stand for? Do they really represent black Americans? For the most part, they toe the line for the liberal agenda of the Democrats. They are pro-abortion, pro-same-sex marriage, and pro-amnesty for illegal immigrants. These people are not my leaders.

Take Maxine Waters. She is a Congresswoman from California and a prominent member of the CBC. Waters was at a recent speech where Louis Farrakhan made racist and anti-Semitic remarks. Has she denounced him? Not a chance. She has a longstanding record of supporting him. And yet, she never misses a chance to criticize President Trump. You could say that she leads the rebellion to impeach President Trump. She is becoming another old face of the "new" Democratic Party on television. And that face is one of hypocrisy and betrayal.

Waters lives in a multi-million-dollar home, a stark contrast to the poor district she represents. She manipulates black voters for her own gain. She's an embarrassment to the black community, and she's just one of many black leaders who has sold out our values. But none of this makes her unique. Instead, Waters is just one of several CBC members who, after years and even decades in Congress, have become multi-millionaires even as the poor districts they represent, sink further into despair. Pay attention to my words. "Woke" needs to wake up.

Let's consider another CBC member, Congressman John Lewis. I marched with Lewis during the civil rights movement. But he questioned the legitimacy of Donald Trump's election and refused to attend the inauguration. At the time, I put out a statement asking Lewis to reconsider. This was the time to heal the country, not stoke division and hatred. I pointed out that Trump had broken the mold of many other modern-day Republicans and asked African Americans to give him a chance. The president deserved that chance. Unfortunately, Lewis put himself on the wrong side of history by ignoring this olive branch and putting politics ahead of principle.

Following President Trump's first State of the Union address where CBC members engaged in rude, juvenile behavior, I joined with other black leaders such as Dr. Alveda King, radio talk host Lonnie Poindexter, and others to demand an apology from the CBC. Black politicians should be concerned with what is important to black Americans — real racism and jobs that will enable black Americans to become independent of the government. Instead, the CBC concerns itself with how to provide more abortions to black women and to protect the rights of people who have entered our country illegally.

Black Lives Matter, Maxine Waters, John Lewis, and others — like Al Sharpton — who claim to be our leaders are a stark reminder that it is time for black Americans to face the truth. The policies embraced by Democrats have been failing us for decades. They have destroyed our communities, weakened our families, and condemned our children to lives of dependency. If the horrific impact of their policies is not enough, Democrats now take our votes for granted as they cater to the abortion industry, radical LGBT rights groups, and illegal immigrants.

These so-called "black leaders" have sold us out!

So how can it be that Democrats can so readily rely on the black vote?

Part of the answer to that question is that Republicans have not reached out to us. Many in the GOP have ignored us. They wrote us off as Democratic voters and decided to spend their time, money, and attention courting others. For this, they should be ashamed. Cutting up America like a demographic pie that will let you piece together power is not leadership. It's politics. If you want to lead the country, then lead. Reach out to everyone. Listen when you're told that you appear not to care about the problems of black Americans. You should do something about it. Democrats didn't take black votes from Republicans. The Republican Party failed to keep black voters.

Another problem with Republicans' appeal to black voters lies in the candidates and what they offer. Many of the GOP politicians have also become "moderate" or — as I see it — prefer not to stand for anything so they can get as many votes as possible from people who don't bother to find out who's on the ballot. When you don't ground your platform in foundational principles, there's no reason for anyone to cross party lines to vote for you.

Even though the Republican Party platform closely matches where most Americans – including black Americans — stand, the GOP is still struggling. As I write this, Republicans control the Senate and the White House, having lost the House. And they may lose power. Why can't they do what they promised their constituents, who are primarily hard-working Americans of faith who love their country?

Do Republicans not realize the many black votes that could be theirs were they to reach out for them? Do Republicans — who once captured most of the black vote — now believe that the massive stranglehold the Democratic Party has on the black vote will last forever? Ecclesiastes states that there is a time and a season for all things. I sincerely believe it's time for a change in the way that black Americans vote. We should vote for the candidates who hold our values. And when you think of the black babies being slaughtered daily by abortion, the black politicians who continue to vote for pro-abortion policies don't deserve our vote.

Unfortunately, African Americans will not begin voting for Republicans if they feel ignored and dismissed by the party. I watched this dismissal of the black vote consistently through Mitt Romney's entire presidential campaign in 2012.

When Romney ran for president against Obama, Karl Rove was his chief man. I met with Reince Priebus — the former chairman of the Republican National Committee — and told him that Rove and Romney were ignoring black people, and that they put black people down. And I'm a Conservative, so I was with Conservatives a lot of the time. I saw this lack of regard consistently and wanted to show that a change could help the GOP regain black votes. But my words fell on deaf ears. They said, "Blacks are not going to vote for us anyway."

But things have changed in the last decade. There is something profoundly different happening now that has never happened before in American history. We can now clearly see the differences between the way the economic structure worked under eight years of America's first black president and two years of President Trump. For the first time in my life, I can see the vast difference in the management of the economy and the effect it has on the pocketbooks of black Americans.

For eight years under President Obama, we kept hearing of the need for jobs programs in the inner cities. We heard about how Republicans refused to vote for government jobs programs. Remember that when President Obama first came into office, Democrats controlled Congress and Republicans could not stop any legislation. In their window of opportunity, did the Democrats try to pass a jobs program for blacks? No. Despite having the power to do so, they did not.

Now after only 30 months in office (at the printing of this book), President Trump has cut regulations, opened energy exploration, and passed tax cuts for businesses and families. Our economy is roaring again! We were told under President Obama that 1-2% growth in our economy was the new normal. We were told that slow growth was all that we, as a mature nation, could achieve. President Trump has taught us that you cannot believe everything you hear in the news.

I am asking black America to listen with their ears and see with their eyes what is happening in the realm of economics. Private companies are placing far more jobs into black America than any government program could do. The invisible hand supporting capitalism will lift black

America when it is not tied down with the regulations and taxes enacted by Democratic Party leaders — including those members of the CBC!

In addition to the problem of indifferent Republicans, we have our problems. Too many black Americans have forgotten the central focus of the message of freedom, which our leaders from the past embraced: the Word of God. When we listen to God's Word and follow His direction for us, we know the path to freedom and how to live as responsible, faith-filled individuals. However, when we are enslaved to politicians who bind us to big government, and to a culture in which celebrity status is glorified, and abortion and same-sex marriage are said to be "civil rights" ... we show we have lost our way to the Promised Land.

Let me be frank about freedom and how easy it is to be led away from it. The Bible tells us how the children of Israel were freed from the bondage of Egypt. They were near the Promised Land. Then, 12 Israeli spies were sent out to survey the Promised Land (Numbers 13:25). Ten spies said the inhabitants were giants and could not be defeated. Two spies said the land could be conquered. You know the rest of the story. The children of Israel had to wander for forty years before a new generation was prepared to conquer the Promised Land.

Black America is near the Promised Land once again. I pray that we do not act like the ten spies who were so afraid that they stood still like a deer in the headlights. Black America, this is not the time to stand still. Now is not the time to keep wandering in the wilderness. As recorded in the book of Deuteronomy, be bold, be strong, and be like Joshua ... be courageous!

Interviewed
by
Laura
Ingraham

4

DO YOU TRULY UNDERSTAND WHAT YOU'RE VOTING FOR?

I believe that at no time since the establishment of the Democratic and Republican parties has there been as stark a difference between the two as there is today. In political circles, cynics commonly say that establishment Republicans and establishment Democrats are the same. But that is not true. Democrats have lurched to the far left in their policies while Republicans are still struggling to decide whether they want to be moderate or fully embrace the constitutional principles on which this nation was founded.

In the Democratic Party, you need to look no further than 28-year-old socialist Alexandria Ocasio-Cortez, who upset a long-time liberal and the fourth most powerful Democrat in the U.S. House of Representatives in the 2018 New York primary. Ocasio-Cortez followed in the footsteps of socialist Bernie Sanders, who could have won the Democratic nomination for President in 2016 if the hierarchy of the Democratic National Committee had not tipped the scales to nominate Hillary Clinton.

When I think of the issues that are important to me — my family, my church, my community — I quickly realize that the Democratic Party platform has moved so far left that it has nothing to offer me. That is why I have urged blacks in America to vote their values.

In their 2016 platform[15], Democrats embraced the Marxist philosophy of redistribution of wealth. They stressed the importance of "economic fairness," with, "rewards that are shared broadly."

Those words certainly sound nice, but that is their purpose — to repackage dangerous policies as attractive and desirable ideas. Remember, in the Bible, when false prophets spoke words to itching ears? For years, the Democratic Party has used wordsmiths to make their rhetoric sound enticing, but have advanced policies that have left our inner cities groaning.

The honeyed words of progressive politics are meant to distract us from their failed ideas. The evidence is right there in front of you. Democrats rule our inner cities and have for over 50 years. Do you like what you see there in Detroit? Chicago? In any of "blue" urban America?

Socialism means forcing higher taxes on Americans who work for a living or have been successful in their lives to pay for "free" services and benefits for those who don't. This philosophy is the basis of most government-run social programs — food stamps, welfare, universal health care, free college tuition, etc. For black Americans, this means that the more the federal government provides so-called "free" services and hand-outs paid for by taxpayers, the more blacks are incentivized to be dependent on the government. With this system, fewer blacks are likely to get an education, work hard for their families, and become entrepreneurs, professionals, and business leaders. With this system, fewer blacks will stand with pride and dignity. Again, look at our numerous inner cities. Do you like what you see?

> The Democrats' socialist system also means that our communities and churches are less likely to help those who are truly in need

The Democrats' socialist system also means that our communities and churches are less likely to help those who are truly in need. Why should they when the government, i.e., taxpayers, will provide all the help they require?

Though many high-level Democratic politicians are extremely wealthy, their platform is filled with rhetoric that sounds as if they are fighting for the working class. They incite resentment of those who have been successful in life, promising to tax them further to provide government-run social programs. For the last 50-or-so years, Democrats have counted on blacks to be the recipients of these "free" government benefits and have labeled any suggestion that these programs be cut as "racist."

To be sure, there are wealthy people who manipulate the tax system to pay less to the government. Just as there are some collecting government welfare and food stamps, and should be out working and supporting their families. Both are wrong. Both are weeds in the capitalist system that divert nutrients from the garden planted for success. In the beautiful garden that is America, these weeds are a distraction and a nuisance.

What socialists don't want you to know is that socialism's appeal is based in one of the seven deadly sins — envy. Socialism wants us to disregard individual achievement and success, claiming that these are somehow "owed" to the many. It counts on the fact that it is human nature to envy the more fortunate and provides a rationale for redistributing their property.

This is a direct repudiation of the spirit of individualism and inquiry that made our country great. America rewards dreamers and innovators. That is the reason for our prosperity. Many of the greatest inventions and ideas that have come to fruition were created by individuals willing to take a risk in a venture to make a profit. Most didn't start wealthy. But if that innovation takes off and the individual's risk is rewarded, he or she can form a company, hire employees, and create jobs for others. This is the American dream.

Jobs are not created by people who do not make a profit. They are created by people whose ideas bring them enough wealth that they can market them and sell their products or services. When they do this, they create jobs for others. I want more black Americans to become entrepreneurs and leaders of innovation and business. I want more black Americans to have jobs and to create jobs for others. If blacks continue to buy into the redistribution of wealth principle of the Democratic Party, we will not be able to participate in a healthy free market economy — a necessity for independent people.

Besides embracing the Marxist economic theory, the Democratic Party's 2016 platform showed the Party reaching out to illegal immigrants and the radical LGBT lobby. Also — and for the first time — Democrats fully embraced abortion and Planned Parenthood, America's largest provider of abortions. Planned Parenthood funds the campaigns of many Democrats and, in turn, demands protection from those elected to office.

On the immigration issue, the Democrats have abandoned black Americans and workers, two groups they supposedly support. There was a time when Democrats advocated for a stop to illegal immigration. Even President Obama spoke of the need for immigration reform. It was understood that unchecked illegal immigration hurts workers at the lower end of the economic spectrum and has a disproportionate effect on black employment.

In recent years, however, the Democratic Party has done an about-face. They have thrown away any pretense of working toward immigration reform. Instead, they advocate for amnesty, oppose any curb on illegal immigration, and make it clear that the goal is to secure a new source of votes. Democrats are behind the establishment of so-called "sanctuary cities" for illegal immigrants.

"We will work to ensure that all Americans — regardless of immigration status — have access to quality health care," the Democrats promised in their platform. "That means expanding community health centers, allowing all families to buy into the Affordable Care Act exchanges, supporting states that open their public health insurance programs to all persons and finally enacting comprehensive immigration reform. And we will expand opportunities for DREAMers to serve in the military and to then receive expedited pathways to citizenship."

"Reforming" the immigration system is one thing, but incentivizing people to come to this country illegally with promises of health care and a sanctuary is undermining the rule of law. How many illegal immigrants does the Democratic Party want to come into America? 10 million? 50 million? 100 million? Unlimited? In many ways, this is what the Democratic Party has come to espouse — overturning our cultural and common-sense norms for their political gain. Just as Democrats have come to take advantage of the black vote in America, they are forging the same relationship with illegal immigrants. Many Democrats are now calling for illegal immigrants to be able to vote — even though they are not U.S. citizens! This is a fraud. And it's exactly how the Democrats hope to remain in power!

As I mentioned earlier, Democrats have allowed the black civil rights movement to be usurped by a radical LGBT lobby that embraces gender ideology — the idea that biology is subservient to and separate from a "chosen" gender. Though it is a scientific fact that there are only two sexes — male and female — the LGBT lobby is attempting to manipulate Americans into believing that people can ignore their biological sex and decide their own gender. "Civil rights" has been expanded to include "sexual orientation" and "gender identity."

When I was fighting to defend traditional marriage, I warned that the politics of the issue went far beyond marriage. Even then, I knew that this was part of a larger effort aimed at dismantling the family. While good, honest people were fooled into thinking that same-sex marriage would not threaten Christian values or institutions, radical activists were preparing to take the next step.

"Democrats applaud last year's decision by the Supreme Court that recognized that LGBT people — like other Americans — have the right to marry the person they love," the Democrats stated in their 2016 platform. In that same year, the Obama administration began pushing to allow boys ("transgender students") into girls' bathrooms in schools across the nation.

Democrats, it seems, are "tolerant" of everyone except Christians. To use their own words:

> Democrats will fight for the continued development of sex discrimination law to cover LGBT people. We will also fight for comprehensive federal non- discrimination protections for all LGBT Americans, to guarantee equal rights in areas such as housing, employment, public accommodations, credit, jury service, education, and federal funding. We will oppose all state efforts to discriminate against LGBT individuals, including legislation that restricts the right to access public spaces. We support a progressive vision of religious freedom that respects pluralism and rejects the misuse of religion to discriminate.

According to the Democrats, if Christians do not support same-sex marriage, they are engaging in, "the misuse of religion to discriminate." While I believe everyone should be treated with respect, I do not have to subjugate my religious belief in marriage between one man and one woman to the Democrats' "progressive vision." The Constitution protects my religious freedom, and I do not have to yield to left-wing ideology to renounce it. Leftist groups like Black Lives Matter frequently call others fascists, yet constantly de-platform their opponents and suppress freedom of speech. I have a right and a duty to speak up like a "Watchman on the Wall" for my family and the people whom I love.

The Democrats have embraced the notion that aborting the unborn is a woman's "right," and they have designed an entire vocabulary that deceives low-information Americans into believing this narrative. Again, in their own words:

> Democrats are committed to protecting and advancing reproductive health, rights, and justice. We believe unequivocally, like many Americans, that every woman should have access to quality reproductive health care services, including safe and legal abortion—regardless of

where she lives, how much money she makes, or how she is insured. We believe that reproductive health is core to women's, men's, and young people's health and wellbeing. We will continue to stand up to Republican efforts to defund Planned Parenthood health centers, which provide critical health services to millions of people. We will continue to oppose — and seek to overturn — federal and state laws and policies that impede a woman's access to abortion, including by repealing the Hyde Amendment. We condemn and will combat any acts of violence, harassment, and intimidation of reproductive health providers, patients, and staff. We will defend the ACA, which extends affordable preventive health care to women, including no-cost contraception, and prohibits discrimination in health care based on gender.

We will support sexual and reproductive health and rights around the globe. In addition to expanding the availability of affordable family planning information and contraceptive supplies, we believe that safe abortion must be part of comprehensive maternal and women's health care and included as part of America's global health programming. Therefore, we support the repeal of harmful restrictions that obstruct women's access to health care information and services, including the "global gag rule" and the Helms Amendment that bars American assistance to provide safe, legal abortion throughout the developing world.

This is the most radical pro-abortion stance I have ever seen! In their platform, the Democrats called for taxpayers to fund abortions — which they refer to as "reproductive justice." Have we come to a point in America where aborting an unborn baby is considered birth control and, worse yet, "justice?"

What would our Founders say? What would Dr. King think if he knew that "justice" in America was defined by some as the right to stop a beating heart in the womb? African American babies are aborted more often than children of any other race or ethnicity. How is this "justice"?

The Democrats also demand "free" contraception for women. Isn't the decision to engage in sexual relations a private one that includes responsibility for its potential outcome? Why should American taxpayers fund people in their decision to have sex? Does the concept of individual responsibility no longer exist for Democrats?

Now, let's look at the Republican Party platform for 2016.[16] The preamble of the platform is a good summary of what I believe about America and its founding. A portion of it is below:

> We believe in American exceptionalism. We believe the United States of America is unlike any other nation on earth.
>
> We believe America is exceptional because of our historic role — first as refuge, then as defender, and now as exemplar of liberty for the world to see.
>
> We affirm — as did the Declaration of Independence: that all are created equal, endowed by their Creator with inalienable rights of life, liberty, and the pursuit of happiness.
>
> We believe in the Constitution as our founding document.
>
> We believe the Constitution was written not as a flexible document, but as our enduring covenant.
>
> We believe our constitutional system — limited government, separation of powers, federalism, and the rights of the people — must be preserved uncompromised for future generations.
>
> We believe political freedom and economic freedom are indivisible. When political freedom and economic freedom are separated — both are in peril; when united, they are invincible.
>
> We believe that people are the ultimate resource — and that the people, not the government, are the best stewards of our country's God-given natural resources.

Where the Democrats embrace the Marxist philosophy of redistribution of wealth – continued taxation for successful people to pay for government-run social programs for others – the Republican party embraces free enterprise with the goal of independence from government. The latter is what blacks need in America to recapture their dignity and pride.

"This is the progressive pathology," the Republicans observed. "Keeping people dependent so that government can redistribute income." They added:

The government cannot create prosperity, though the government can limit or destroy it. Prosperity is the product of self-discipline, enterprise, saving, and investment by individuals, but it is not an end. Prosperity provides how citizens and their families can maintain their independence from government, raise their children by their values, practice their faith, and build communities of cooperation and mutual respect. It is also the foundation for our nation's global leadership, for it is the vigor of our economy, which makes possible our military strength and our national security.

Earlier, we saw how the seeds of the effort to establish equality for all Americans ultimately brought forth fruit. The work of father and son John and John Quincy Adams, Benjamin Franklin, and Thomas Jefferson came to fruition in the determination of Republican President Abraham Lincoln to abolish slavery and in the conviction of Dr. Martin Luther King, Jr. to free blacks from oppression through a peaceful movement.

This is what Republicans had to say in their 2016 platform about the founding of our country:

We are the party of the Declaration of Independence and the Constitution. The Declaration sets forth the fundamental precepts of American government: That God bestows certain inalienable rights on every individual. Thus producing human equality; that government exists first and foremost to protect those inalienable rights; that man-made law must be consistent with God-given, natural rights; and that if God-given, natural, inalienable rights come in conflict with government, court, or human-granted rights, God-given, natural, inalienable rights always prevail. There is a moral law recognized as "the Laws of Nature and, of Nature's God"; and that American government is to operate with the consent of the governed.

Yes, "God-given, natural rights," should prevail over government-granted rights, and there is an inherent, natural "moral law" — created by God – that is recognized in our Constitution. Blacks have always believed this, and those who have been our true leaders took God's word with them. The Declaration of Independence and the Constitution — because they are founded on Judeo-Christian principles —

are a natural extension of what we believe about God and our relationship with Him.

The Republicans continued:

> We reaffirm the Constitution's fundamental principles: limited government, separation of powers, individual liberty, and the rule of law. We denounce bigotry, racism, anti-Semitism, ethnic prejudice, and religious intolerance. Therefore, we oppose discrimination based on race, sex, religion, creed, disability, or national origin and support statutes to end such discrimination. As the Party of Abraham Lincoln, we must continue to foster solutions to America's difficult challenges when it comes to race relations today. We continue to encourage equality for all citizens and access to the American Dream. Merit and hard work should determine advancement in our society, so we reject unfair preferences, quotas, and set-asides as forms of discrimination. Our ranks include Americans from every faith and tradition, and we respect the right of each American to follow his or her deeply held beliefs.

These are the things that I believe and that I think most blacks believe. My parents taught me to become educated and work hard to achieve my goals, and this is what I have taught my children as well. I want to be judged on the work I do, and I don't want to be given special preferences or privileges because of the color of my skin — nobody should. Racial quotas and affirmative action are forms of discrimination because they are based on the notion that blacks can't possibly compete with whites in education or business. That couldn't be further from the truth. Keep reading because later in this book, I will tell you how we can end racism now.

As we have seen, Democrats have tried to control the narrative on illegal immigration, hoping to ensure those who come to this country illegally will keep them in power. They now refer to these individuals as "undocumented" instead of "illegal" and claim Republicans are cruel and harsh for wanting to abide by our nation's immigration laws.

Here is what Republicans have to say about immigration. Notice how they distinguish between "legal" and "illegal" immigrants and frame their argument in terms of what is best for "American working families and their wages." That, of course, includes black Americans:

> Our party is the natural home for those who come in search of freedom and justice. We welcome all to the Great Opportunity Party. The greatest asset of the American economy is the American worker. Our immigration system must protect American working families and their wages, for citizens and legal immigrants alike, in a way that will improve the economy. Just as immigrant labor helped build our country in the past, today's legal immigrants are making vital contributions in every aspect of national life. Their industry and commitment to American values strengthens our economy, enriches our culture, and enables us to understand better and more effectively compete with the rest of the world...
>
> America's immigration policy must serve the national interest of the United States, and the interests of American workers must be protected over the claims of foreign nationals seeking the same jobs.

Republicans, you will also see, have a starkly different view of marriage from that of the Democrats:

> Foremost among [our] institutions is the American family. It is the foundation of civil society, and the cornerstone of the family is natural marriage, the union of one man and one woman. Its daily lessons — cooperation, patience, mutual respect, responsibility, self-reliance — are fundamental to the order and progress of our Republic. Strong families, depending upon God and one another, advance the cause of liberty by lessening the need for government in their daily lives. Conversely, as we have learned over the last five decades, the loss of faith and family life leads to greater dependence upon government.

In many ways, this is the core of what my message is in this book. Since a significant number of blacks became subservient to the government and its hand-outs, our families have disintegrated, and fewer have fathers in the home. Too many of our black children are involved in crime and drugs — so many of them have died due to gang violence or now sit in prison. When our families are broken, so too are our communities and our neighborhood schools. Black children who want to learn cannot do so in chaotic or dangerous environments. The value of hard work cannot be taught to children when their parents are dependent on government welfare. Where are the role models for our black children?

"Every child deserves a married mom and dad," the Republican platform said. I wholeheartedly agree that a mother and father, raising their children together, is the keyway for blacks to get to that Promised Land.

On the issue of the sanctity of human life, once again, the difference between Republicans and Democrats is glaring. The Republicans said in their platform:

> We support a human life amendment to the Constitution and legislation to make clear that the Fourteenth Amendment's protections apply to children before birth.

> We oppose the use of public funds to perform or promote abortion or to fund organizations, like Planned Parenthood, so long as they provide or refer for elective abortions or sell fetal body parts rather than provide healthcare. We urge all states and Congress to make it a crime to acquire, transfer, or sell fetal tissues from elective abortions for research, and we call on Congress to enact a ban on any sale of fetal body parts. In the meantime, we call on Congress to ban the practice of misleading women on so-called fetal harvesting consent forms, a fact revealed by a 2015 investigation. We will not fund or subsidize healthcare that includes abortion coverage. We support the appointment of judges who respect traditional family values and the sanctity of innocent human life.

Life, marriage, family, faith — these are my values. Can you see why I've encouraged blacks to vote their values? I want to see our black community grow stronger and more prosperous, and I want to see family and faith respected and preserved. When I saw the values of the Democratic Party reflected in their politics and platform, I concluded that the Democratic Party no longer has room for me. I have realized that my relationship with the Democrats was completely one-sided. They asked for everything — support, votes, loyalty. And they gave nothing in return.

This is not to suggest that the Republicans are without flaw. Although I believe the Republican platform consists of ideas and goals that are closer to my own, some

Republican politicians don't abide by their Party's platform. Some prefer to appear "moderate" on many of the issues to attract a wider array of voters. That is why it is important for black Americans not to vote for candidates just because they have "D" after their names ... or even an "R." We must all educate ourselves about candidates running for office and vote for the person whose values and philosophy are closest to our own.

At this crossroads in history, these party platforms show the stark differences between the Republican Party and the Democratic Party. And just as the Democratic Party made a sharp left turn and removed many of the values I believe in -- the Republican Party has been trying to preserve those values. I have friends who were at the 2016 Republican National Convention. I am told that there were forces fighting to "tone down" the Judeo-Christian values written into the Republican platform, especially concerning marriage and abortion. But the Republican leaders on the platform committee continually fought for the most conservative and values-supported Republican platform that has ever been written. These opposing forces are not going away.

The same forces that effectively removed God from the Democratic platform are attacking our Christian rights. Many of you reading this will not want to admit this truth. I fear that the Democratic Party is too far gone, but if you choose to stay, I ask you to fight for what our Christian values. Do not let the Democratic leaders put you in the "back of the bus." I have seen black leaders who fight for life and marriage removed from leadership positions within the Democratic Party. Please fight to change your party if you remain a Democrat — but be ready to stand for your Christian convictions if the Democrats try to muzzle your freedom of speech!

The progressive forces now attacking the Republican Party can be easily defeated with one major change. Put God first. Bring God back into our daily lives and decisions. The future of God-promoted values in America can have its greatest influence if both major parties fight for righteousness. But if the Democratic Party continues to resist biblical values, then the most powerful force for those values will be black Christians working to restore our Christian values.

The forces working against biblical values in both parties can be counteracted by "We the People" fighting to restore Godly principles. There's a poetry in the way this would let the Republican Party come full circle. The GOP formed to free the slaves. Now it needs the great-grandsons and great-granddaughters of these once-enslaved people to fortify the biblical foundations of our great Republic!

Let me say that in this day of misinformation, distortion, and division, I am not ashamed to call myself a conservative. Progressives and leftists try to affiliate conservatives with racism. They want to make the two words synonyms — but they are flat out wrong!

I think of myself as a conservative. I think of myself in that way because of the influence of my home and church, not because of political or party affiliation.

I am also a conservative because I care about scriptural living, not merely scriptural quotation. Anyone can quote the Bible, and there are demagogues who judiciously select words and phrases from Scripture while simultaneously advancing an ungodly agenda.

I am a conservative because I care about family values lived — not merely family values voiced. Family values begin with valuing the family. And what is a family? It begins with one man and one woman and includes their children, biological or adopted.

I was raised in a God-fearing, committed family, and it is from my family that I obtained my convictions. My parents helped me to form my convictions through their teachings, and they provided me with exposure to the Scriptures and the guidance of pastors and religious leaders in our community.

I am a conservative because I care about individual choice, not merely public conformity. And I care about genuine diversity, not merely group membership. I believe everyone should be free to choose their friends, their neighborhood, their children's schools, their candidates for election, and the way they worship God. Conservatives respect individual choice and individual opinion. And they support the right to disagree.

> I am a conservative because I care about individual choice, not merely public conformity

Finally, I am a conservative because I care about human dignity, not merely about human glory. A selfish desire for glory generates a willingness to undermine genuine human dignity. Everyone possesses dignity. Even unborn infants have dignity, although they have little human glory. The old and the sick have the divine dignity that God gave them, and this dignity has remained undimmed even in the fading light of human glory.

I am a conservative!

Reverend Owens to African American leaders to Give Trump a chance

5

GIVE ME A CHANCE TO BE EDUCATED

W hen I was growing up, blacks suffered many injustices. Imagine what it would be like if the color of your skin placed you at an immediate disadvantage. That was my life growing up in Memphis, Tennessee, during the Jim Crow era. As a boy and as a young man, I lived a segregated life in a segregated city and state. I knew anger and despair, but faith in God — and a mother and father who loved me — made all the difference. My mother encouraged all of us to get an education, and we did.

Today, despite the insurmountable odds that black men faced 50 years ago, I am both a minister and an educator. Did I suffer racial prejudice? Yes. But, so did millions of other blacks. We were determined to make something of our lives, and we persevered and went to college. Many blacks became doctors, lawyers, nurses, educators, politicians, inventors, philanthropists, musicians, entertainers, journalists, entrepreneurs ... in short, every profession available in this great country. I have had the opportunity to sit and learn at the feet of many wise men and women, including Bishop J.O. Patterson, Sr., the late presiding bishop of the Church of God in Christ, Dr. Oral Roberts, inspiring teachers, and my principal, Mr. Blair T. Hunt. They all taught me valuable lessons. Mr. Hunt, like my mother, gave us confidence and made us proud to be black. She would say, "You can be black as 50,000 midnights, but be somebody."

> She would say, "You can be black as 50,000 midnights, but be somebody"

Nevertheless, I was an "at-risk" student who grew up during segregation and doubted my ability to go to college. With the benefit of hindsight, I can see that my hardships were part of a journey. They gave me a deeper understanding of the challenges faced by young "at-risk" men and women who share that same uncertainty about their future. Thus, when God called, I was ready. In December 1988, when I was in seminary and finally heard God's plan for me, I started an organization to help students who had a desire to attend college but had little chance of gaining entry. The Give Me a Chance Ministry (GMAC) provided at-risk students with a chance to study at a premier university.

Many of the students we served in GMAC did not meet the rigorous academic standards of Oral Roberts University (ORU), but we were able to stand in the gap and ask the university to give them a chance. We placed no demands on the university but asked them to help students who otherwise may not have had the opportunity to receive a college education.

GMAC succeeded more than anyone could have expected. In only four years, we were able to increase the black enrollment at ORU from 5 percent to 22.5 percent. There's a critical lesson to be had in that success rate. At GMAC, we didn't think that our work was accomplished simply by getting at-risk students into the school. We were there to help young men and women succeed, and that included giving them the tools and support that might have been missing from their lives before. That's why we also provided tutoring, mentoring, and scholarships for many of our students.

Our efforts were not directed only at black students. We helped at-risk students from all backgrounds and socio-economic levels. Many of these students are successful today because of the opportunity and access we afforded them through our partnership with ORU — to which we are forever grateful for embracing our efforts and giving students a chance to succeed.

When I think about what we were trying to do to help "at-risk" students — to better themselves, to follow their dreams, to become independent, and, as Mr. Hunt would say, to be somebody – then witness what has become of many black Americans, I'm filled with an unbelievable sadness.

Just think. We are only four generations away from slavery, but blacks are being coerced into a new form of slavery. This modern state of dependence puts the government in the role of master/ benefactor. But that sense of reliance is there. They still must depend on the "master;" on somebody other than themselves.

We, however, grew up in a time when you depended on yourself. You had to to make it. When you depend on other people, you do away with your ability to solve problems and deal with your situation.

I still remember the day I went to observe a food stamp office. What I saw was upsetting. Young non-disabled young people were walking in, saying, "I want my food stamps." No sense of regret or self-consciousness about the fact that they were dependent on someone else for their very sustenance. What they were getting from the government was a handout, but there was no sense of awareness that they were devaluing their worth by participating in this cycle of dependence. The sense of pride and self-reliance that George Washington Carver had demonstrated when he said, "I never allowed anyone to give me money, no difference how badly I needed it. I wanted literally to earn my living," had disappeared. At some point in the last century, the knowledge that dependance is a slow-poison disappeared. Sadly, that's the mindset that has been passed on since the civil rights movement. (*See Appendix B, Home/Family*)

I have eight children — six of them grown. One thing I do not have in my family is a lazy child. My children were made to get up in the morning. They had chores at home, and they had to go to school. They were trained to work. At an early age, they sold apples and pencils to learn about working for payment.

I wanted my children to learn to provide for themselves, and I didn't want them to be spoiled or entitled. More than that, however, I wanted them to know their self-worth — that they are capable, intelligent, and able to accomplish anything. Unfortunately, we are not passing those lessons on to the younger generation, and it shows. I can't help but notice that many blacks have bought into the culture of handouts and entitlement, and it is sapping our sense of initiative and self-reliance. Our people may have been freed from slavery over 150 years ago, but many have enslaved themselves again to government programs and progressive politicians.

The creation and development of GMAC are one of my proudest accomplishments. One of the most important features of this early effort was how it was achieved through my work with pastors, parents, students, and church leaders. I was able to build strong relationships and an effective network that would span the country.

My organization – the Coalition of African-American Pastors (CAAP)[17] — grew out of that network. Through CAAP, we address the full spectrum of threats to the family, from education reform to transgender rights. Using a combination of media savvy and the network that was established long ago with the Give Me a Chance Ministry, I continue to strive to make a real difference in the fight to save the soul of our nation.

GMAC also holds a special place in my heart because it was through that ministry that I met my wife, Deborah, and we began our journey as husband and wife and our mission to achieve our goal of educating black Americans.

After GMAC, Deborah created Education for All. This program expanded the effort to create new opportunities for youth and includes other universities, colleges, and technical schools. It's our goal to inspire, educate, and empower students through initiatives like our Achievers Program, through which we encourage, teach, and mentor emerging hard workers as they build success on principles of virtue.

Black Americans are at a crossroad. Over the last 50 years, they have been subjected to a nearly relentless campaign of manipulation — in truth, it is more like an attempt to brainwash us. To resist it, blacks must become more educated about politics. That's why I'm writing this book and why Deborah and I are on this journey.

> More than anything, I want black Americans to embrace self-reliance as the path to success

More than anything, I want black Americans to embrace self-reliance as the path to success. Relying on the government comes with the loss of a certain amount of dignity. Black America will never be truly free until the dream of financial independence is achieved. Allegiance to the Democratic Party for 50 years has now failed us.

The so-called safety net has been turned into a low-budget hammock too many times. We do need a safety net, but for those who can work, the safety net should never be converted into a hammock. We cannot wave a magic wand or design a silver bullet to solve all our problems. But we can begin working together to make sure we encourage each other on this journey to the Promised Land.

Prayer is very important, but prayer alone won't help blacks choose the right path. The truth is that we need a combination of prayer, faith, and action. Deborah and I will continue to help black Americans by carrying the torch of freedom and lighting the way for their hopes and dreams to become a reality. Dr. King said that he might not get there with us, but we will get to the Promised Land. Keep on reading because the best is yet to come.

24th year anniversary

6

DEBORAH'S TURN: A FEDERAL ROLE IN EDUCATION HAS NOT HELPED BLACK CHILDREN

I arrived in the United States from Panama at 12 years of age. My parents wanted more for their children, and they saw America as the land of opportunity — flowing with "milk and honey." Indeed, it is. Like many immigrants, I achieved more in America than I could have dreamed, and I will be forever grateful for this land of opportunity. I proudly became an American citizen on September 22, 2000.

I finished middle school, high school, and earned a bachelor's degree here in the United States. Eventually, I earned my doctorate in education from Vanderbilt University. For a young girl who began life in a Third World country, America meant freedom from poverty and lack. It also meant freedom of opportunity and freedom to dream. And America meant freedom to learn.

In 1991, I was working in New York City in the advertising industry and trying to figure out my personal life when I heard about a Lindsay Roberts Women's Conference. I immediately felt inspired to attend.

During one session of the conference, Lindsay spoke about the Give Me a Chance (GMAC) ministry and its goal of recruiting, matriculating and providing scholarships to Oral Roberts University (ORU) students. I knew God was leading me to attend ORU, so, without knowing how I would support myself financially, I resigned from my job and headed to Tulsa, Oklahoma.

Soon after I arrived at ORU, I attended a study skills seminar sponsored by GMAC and met the staff and many students. I was able to get a student work-study job working for GMAC while I worked hard on my studies. Eventually, my hard work paid off, and I graduated on time!

It was at ORU that I met my husband, Bill. He was an evangelist for education back then. If young people weren't in school, he would ask, "Why aren't you in school?" and tell them, "I'll get you in school." A lot of young black people were admitted on probation. Bill signed on those students, and we would mentor and tutor them.

Now, I am the president of Education for All[18] and its subdivision, Mission Education. We launched Mission Education because we believe two critical components are missing from ongoing discussions around national education reform: families and communities. Schools alone cannot fix the problems we are seeing in K-12 students. And all too often, these problems keep them from becoming productive members of society.

Students attending public schools in the United States are either stagnating or falling behind.

Test scores released in 2018 from the National Assessment of Educational Progress (NAEP)[19] — also known as the Nation's Report Card — show that 65 percent of the eighth-graders in American public schools in 2017 were not proficient in reading, and 67 percent were not proficient in mathematics. If this news is not bad enough, the NAEP test results are even worse for students in some inner-city school districts – mostly black and Hispanic children.

The city of Detroit, Michigan, for example, showed the lowest percentage of students who scored at the proficient level or higher in both mathematics and reading. Test results from that city saw only 5 percent of eighth-graders proficient or higher in math and only 7 percent performing similarly in reading.

The news is not much better in other big cities.

In Cleveland, Ohio, only 11 percent of students in eighth grade were at proficiency level or higher in math, and only 10 percent reached proficiency level in reading.

Only 11 percent of eighth-graders in Baltimore, Maryland public schools were proficient or higher in math and only 14 percent in reading.

We also see another pattern affecting many black children. The 2018 NAEP test results showed that, in general, higher-performing fourth-grade students remained relatively flat on both mathematics and reading, but lower-performing students declined even further. This means that students from lower socio-economic groups, like many black children, dropped further in their test scores, leaving a much wider achievement gap between white and black students.

These test results come at a time when the Common Core State Standards — a federally incentivized education reform — have been in effect in most states for five to seven years. Billions of dollars in both taxpayer and private money went into developing and implementing the Common Core, and the tests aligned with them. Yet, we still see no improvement.

Keep in mind that former President Barack Obama criticized the country for the continued achievement gap between white and minority children. His answer was more federal involvement in education. But years later, we see that increased government intervention in education not only hasn't improved the situation; it has left students struggling even more.

Recent international test results released by the National Center for Education Statistics (NCES) also show that children in our country keep falling further behind their peers in other nations. On another assessment, the Progress in International Reading Literacy Study, United States fourth graders have dropped from fifth in the international rankings in 2011 to 13th in 2016 out of 58 international education systems.

"We seem to be declining as other education systems record larger gains on the assessment," said Peggy G. Carr, acting commissioner for the federal NCES, according to the Washington Post.[20] "This is a trend we've seen on other international assessments in which the U.S. participates."

Each time another standardized test yields disappointing results; however, progressives fill the media with demands for higher taxes, so more federal funding can be funneled to public schools. Teachers unions then demand higher pay. And wealthy philanthropists who think they have the solution join with government officials to create yet another school reform initiative to close "the achievement gap" between middle- and lower-income children.

A seminal 1983 report titled A Nation at Risk[21] revealed the dismal state of our nation's education system and emphasized accountability. However, the increased accountability and the "governing" of education has placed an undue burden on teachers and schools and has shifted the focus to a one-size-fits-all approach to education. The individual child has gotten lost in all this government "intervention." (*For more data, see Appendix B, Education.*)

> The system isn't just failing students; it's failing teachers as well

The system isn't just failing students; it's failing teachers as well. Search social media, and you can easily find accounts from teachers explaining why they're leaving the profession. Often, they'll cite a preoccupation with training, technology, and government benchmarks that is taking them out of the classroom.

The bureaucratization of education has been a boon to bureaucrats and consultants, but it's made things worse for students and educators.

Part of the problem is the mistaken belief that the solution to our education woes can be crafted and enforced from Washington, D.C. All students are entitled to a fair and equal education. However, funding, quality teachers, and curriculum aren't the primary factors for student achievement.

Without strong parental and community involvement, increasing and sustaining student achievement is highly unlikely. Students must be able to make positive connections in the school setting, community setting, and (of course) at home.

Many big government politicians think they know what black American children need to succeed in school. The truth is, however, that black children did far better in their neighborhood schools before integration. In those schools, despite the access and equity issues of the time, students made important connections with the school itself as well as their greater community. Neighborhood churches were also more involved in public schools before religion was pushed out of the public square.

While progressive politicians and so-called "experts" focus on government intervention to solve the problem of failing education, they are missing are the most important pieces for children – parents and communities.

Unfortunately, those same progressives have espoused "social justice" policies that have gutted black communities. A multitude of single mothers, children with no fathers, and families dependent on government assistance have become the norm rather than the exception in many of our black communities. When children have no mother-father team as their first educators, society expects schools to pick up the slack and take on more of the parenting role.

To break this cycle, parents and communities must be engaged in the education process. This is the key to creating an environment that pushes students to succeed — especially low-income students.

Parents are a child's first teachers — not the government at any level. And it is not the role of the federal government to "govern" what's best for schools around the nation.

To keep parents involved in their children's education, decisions should be made at the local level, where parents and communities can have an impact.

Parents and communities are what help students succeed in school and life. To say the federal government is more concerned or knows more about what's best for my child's education than I do is absurd and an insult. And for black parents to expect government schools to provide everything for their children is also an insult – to those children.

> Churches should embrace new ways to be a part of the education process through the internet and computers

Rather than more government, we need more education options for families. We also need a concerted effort to involve more churches and community members in the teaching of students, particularly our black children. We should look forward to the new technology that will change the way we educate children and adults. Churches should embrace new ways to be a part of the education process through the internet and computers. We have a bright future in education. Don't fear God-inspired innovation — be a part of it!

Deborah
Owens
Shares

7

THE DESTRUCTION OF THE BLACK FAMILY IN AMERICA

Strong families — with mothers and fathers working together to raise their children — are at the center of cultures that nurture, educate, and promote faith, the dignity of human life, and hard work. Sadly, blacks in America are suffering because of the disintegration of our families. As we will see, without strong families, our culture cannot prevail.

When I was growing up, we were poor. But we worked hard and never thought about getting welfare from the government. My mother and father taught us to get an education and get a job so that we could provide for ourselves. And they weren't unusual in doing so. Even under an unfair, discriminatory system, black Americans didn't make excuses. We were a people of pride and dignity. Our families were strong, and most black children had their mothers and fathers raising them together, teaching them how to be the best they could. Sadly, the mindset of many black Americans has changed considerably since that time and not, I believe, for the better.

When I hear blacks speak disparagingly of President Donald Trump, I must ask, "Why?" What did Obama do for us, except make the government bigger and put more of our people on food stamps? Obama continued what Lyndon Johnson set out to do — make blacks more dependent on government. Trump, however, wants blacks to be back in the workforce because he knows that when people are working and taking responsibility for themselves and putting food on the tables for their families, they are ultimately happier, better off, and more in control of their lives.

> Obama continued what Lyndon Johnson set out to do — make blacks more dependent on government

In the past two years, I've urged people to give President Trump a chance, and I've defended the president against those who would attack him and distort his record. Personally, I'm not interested in the political battles and name-calling that have characterized the last few years. What matters to me is that President Trump did what he promised. He defended life, protected freedom of religion, and improved economic conditions for all Americans.

It must also be said that it wasn't the first black president who reached out to my fellow pastors and me for help enacting prison reform; it was President Trump. Time and again, he reached out to black pastors and the black community to seek our assistance and show us that he cares about our issues.

Regardless of what people think about Trump's personality, he is the President of the United States, and all of us — black, brown, or white — should respect his office. Even though I did not support most of President Obama's policies during his presidency, I always respected the elected office that he held. When I hear people say that Trump is not their president, then I want to ask, "What country are you from?" We are Americans, and under our Constitution, we can have only one president elected by the people every four years.

Thanks to the biased and divisive news media, many blacks have fallen for the myth that President Trump somehow won a flawed election. Apparently, they have forgotten that President Obama was in charge during that election. And it was Obama who said that, with our decentralized election process, no one could rig our elections (even if they wanted to). If you were a Hillary Clinton supporter, I ask you to do for Trump what I did for the underprivileged students nobody thought could succeed in college — give him a chance!

There's a good reason for black Democrats to give President Trump a chance to prove worthy of their trust. Not only has he acted on issues that directly affect the black community, like abortion and prison reform, but he has also helped put more money in black homes by boosting the economy and lowering black unemployment.

The federal government's Bureau of Labor Statistics[22] says the May 2018 unemployment rate for blacks aged 16 and over is 5.9 percent. That's the lowest it has been since the government started collecting such data in 1972 — 46 years ago! And this figure has been dropping since January 2018. Think about it. Fewer blacks are unemployed than at any time since they started gathering this data, and it is happening in the age of Donald Trump — not Barack Obama!

Some try to claim that President Trump is riding on the great economy that President Obama created. Unfortunately, that's just partisanship talking. The facts tell a different story. Did Obama's strategy of increasing regulations and taxes lead to more than 1 or 2% growth? No. You can opine all you want, but you cannot ignore the fact that there are more opportunities for those graduating from college and coming out of prisons. That job growth did not happen because of eight years of President Obama. Our robust economy is due to the policies of President Trump. (*See Appendix B, Labor and Business.*)

Stop, "drinking the Kool-Aid." See with your eyes and hear with your ears and listen to the people who have more job opportunities and more ladders to success than I can ever remember. For years, we heard the constant refrain that the only way to provide opportunities for young people is to create government jobs for them, especially in black communities. Under Trump's economy, young people aged 16-24 have more job opportunities than they have had in over 50 years. Reward success when you go to the ballot box. Stop wasting your votes on politicians and policies that have failed us since the 1960s!

This is one of the main reasons why I, Bill Owens, endorsed Trump for president (as an individual, not as CAAP) in 2016. I didn't mind sharing about why we should give Trump a chance. He didn't ignore blacks, unlike Mitt Romney!

The Democratic Party has offered black Americans nothing but failed policies and empty promises. Meanwhile, Donald Trump has asked blacks to give him a chance. When he launched his 2016 campaign, Trump was in the same situation as I was when I was running the Give Me a Chance Ministry. Our goal was to provide scholarships, to tutor, and to mentor students who wouldn't otherwise be able to get a college education. What was key to the success of that program was the fact that we asked nothing from the university other than that they give our students a chance to succeed. That is what Trump was asking of blacks when he ran for president. And after witnessing 50 years of failure from Democrats — who have grown to become enemies of the dignity of every human life as well as opponents of religious liberty– I believed it was time to give Trump the chance he asked for to prove he could be a great president.

> I believed it was time to give Trump the chance he asked for to prove he could be a great president

When I decided to endorse Trump, I wrote an open letter[23] to black voters.

"You likely voted for Democrats in the past — possibly because you were told that the Democratic Party is 'for' African Americans," I said. "And you may be considering voting Democrat again, even though you don't like the nominee. I am here to ask you to think again. Now is the time for African American voters to vote their values!"

In my letter to black Americans, I said it was time we faced the truth, and I still mean that almost three years later. The truth we must face is that the Democrats have destroyed our communities, weakened our families, and doomed us to a future of dependency. Plus, the Democrats take our votes for granted as they cater to interest groups like the abortion industry, the radical LGBT lobby, and illegal immigrants.

The truth we must face is that blacks became enslaved to welfare and government entitlement programs with Lyndon Johnson's Great Society. The Democrats knew that if we became dependent on government, we would no longer be asking them, "Where are the jobs for our people?" What happened next is an embarrassment. We lost our motivation to work hard and succeed. We lost our determination to keep our families proud and strong. What the Democrats did to us was destroy our dignity at a time when it should have been flourishing. And they also destroyed the black family as we knew it. Let me show you how that happened.

President Lyndon Johnson enacted the food stamp program in 1964 as part of his Great Society plan.

When Congress created food stamps, thousands of welfare recruiters were sent into cities across the nation to sign up low-income mothers for government welfare and food stamps. In *Liberal Fascism*[24], Jonah Goldberg wrote about the targeted nature of this campaign: "James Bovard notes that when Congress mandated food stamps, welfare 'recruiters' — a hundred thousand of them created by the War on Poverty — went into the cities to convince poor people to enroll."

Yes — it's high time we face the truth. Many black Americans didn't just "turn to" food stamps because they were poor. In fact, blacks resisted government help. The Johnson administration worked to recruit black Americans to sign onto the food stamp program.

As Bishop Harry R. Jackson observed[25] at Townhall in February 2013, the United States Department of Agriculture (USDA) magazine reported happily in 1972 that, "With careful explanations . . . coupled with intensive outreach efforts, resistance from the 'too prouds' is bending."

Yes, most black people in the 1960s were "too proud" to accept government hand-outs, and blacks turned their backs on the program. This wasn't what the government wanted. They needed people on the welfare rolls, and they wanted black Americans to cave, to sign up for government dependency. Initially, our dignity and resolve protected us. But once the savvy welfare recruiters appealed to black parents by claiming the government subsidies were for their children, blacks caved, and the recruiters knew they had broken their pride.

But this scheme to create a generation dependent on government hand-outs didn't stop in the 1960s. During the presidential administrations of Bill Clinton and Barack Obama, the federal government continued to recruit blacks for the food stamp program.

The Washington Post noted[26] in 2013 that the USDA launched extensive outreach programs to sign more people onto food stamps during the Obama administration. Some states even hired food stamp recruiters who were required to fill a quota each month of new food stamp enrollees. "Food Stamps Make America Stronger," was the Obama administration's line.

Recruiters were trained to deal with people who said "no" to food stamps because they didn't want to be on government welfare. The Post story told of one Florida recruiter's trained response to an older man, who resisted her pitch to sign up for food stamps. He told her, "I don't want to be another person depending on the government."

"How about being another person getting the help you deserve?" the recruiter shot back at him.

The help you deserve? This is what has happened to many black Americans. We have bought into this twisted mindset that we "deserve" hand-outs. And because we "deserve" them and they are "owed" to us, we should not have to work for them. This is total rubbish! Do you see how political manipulation has caused black America to go from "proud" and "dignified" to dependent on government? (*For more, see Appendix B, Government Assistance.*)

I grew up during a time when blacks were indeed "proud." And we had a lot to be proud of. We were hard workers, striving to do what was best for our families. You can be sure that dependency on government is one thing that has prevented blacks from entering the Promised Land of freedom.

The Clinton administration also engaged in this effort to create a dependent mindset. In 2000, Clinton broadened the eligibility requirements for food stamps by allowing states to raise minimum income limits so that more people could sign up. And in 2009, the Obama administration ended food stamp work requirements, even for those able to work.[27]

Just about half of eligible Americans were enrolled in the food stamp program in 2003. But in 2013, during the Obama administration, 75 percent of those eligible signed up. By that year, a record 47.6 million Americans were relying on food stamps! In fact, under Obama, you could be on food stamps even if you had a large bank account because of expanded eligibility criteria.[28] What message did that send to Americans? The message I heard was, "You don't need to work to take care of your family. Be dependent on government. Keep voting for us, and we'll keep giving you those hand-outs."[29]

Now let's compare this to the data for the Trump administration. The latest USDA data shows that in February 2017 — one month after Donald Trump was inaugurated — food stamp enrollment was at 42.3 million. In May 2018, however, participation in the food stamp program dropped to 40 million. More than two million got off the food stamp rolls in a little more than a year under Trump. The USDA under Trump also released a plan that would enact work requirements for those who receive food stamps and can work. Of course, as expected, the Democrats complained about this, attempting to portray Trump as "heartless."[30] But why should people who are capable of working receive welfare?

Government dependency helped create the issues in black America that we see today. Untold thousands of single mothers with multiple children — many from different fathers, and all on welfare — are raising their children without fathers in the home. With the government incentivizing women to remain single by providing welfare subsidies and food stamps for single mothers, black men were no longer a part of the family. Many young black women continued to have children to increase their welfare payments. Black men, who once worked to support their families and provided authority and stability in their homes, are no longer around serving as role models for our black sons.

As more young boys grew up without fathers, they lacked the foundation fathers provide. Many have turned to life in the streets with gangs, drugs, and crime – looking for the guidance and authority that a father provides. The prisons have become filled with young black boys, and everything that brought pride and dignity to many black families has disappeared. The effect on our families, communities, and culture has been devastating. (*See Appendix B, Home/Family.*)

I see the statistics that show how many black men are incarcerated; these statistics are often used to declare that our justice system is racist. How is it that after eight years, President Obama left us with a racist justice system? If our justice system is racist, then blame President Obama, Eric Holder, and Loretta Lynch. They had eight years to make it right.

In all honesty, however, those statistics may not be explained by racism. The same statistics could show that most people in prison — regardless of the color of their skin — generally grew up without a father in the home. Is it racist to not have a father in the home? It is disappointing not to have a father in the home, but it cannot be called racist.

The black family was the cornerstone of black America, and now many have lost that critical foundation! We must restore black fathers as the bedrock to our culture. Our black children can be the generation that achieves the freedom that is the Promised Land, but we can't delay in showing them the way.

Fathers remain committed to your children. Young black people everywhere, be responsible and do not have children until you are ready to provide a home with a mother and a father. Let us fully grasp biblical principles and live them out to enjoy blessed lives. Financial freedom for black America starts in our homes, and it means making common sense, biblically-based decisions.

29th year anniversary

8

THE DESTRUCTION OF MARRIAGE IN AMERICA AND THE RISE OF TRANSGENDERISM

W e cannot have strong families without placing a value on the distinct roles mothers and fathers hold in the lives of their children. Marriage between a man and a woman is the bond from which comes the strength to nurture and educate children together.

As we have seen, the Democrats have "redefined" marriage to include same-sex marriage. They glorify single mothers and even discourage marriage through increased government welfare and other benefits if women remain single.

I have shown you how the Democratic Party has come to rely on the black vote, yet its political platform has grown radically liberal, and it has become anti-faith, anti-family, and hostile to religious liberty. Blacks continue voting for Democrats even though the platform doesn't reflect their values, much to the advantage of the Party.

Democrats, though they expect blacks to vote for them in every election, have undermined us and our most dearly-held religious beliefs. One of those is marriage.

The black Church has always held marriage between a man and a woman as holy and created by God. Not only did Obama dismiss our religious belief in marriage, but he did so by using our civil rights movement to undermine it.

Consider our struggle during that movement — our struggle to be treated with dignity and respect as all people should. I am outraged and insulted that Democrats have tossed blacks aside — blacks who were once enslaved, lynched, spat upon, and made to drink water out of separate fountains from whites — by allowing radical LGBT lobbying groups to usurp our movement.

> The black Church has always held marriage between a man and a woman as holy and created by God

The Obama administration's decision to push same-sex marriage and transgender bathrooms on the nation — and liken these to equality for blacks during the civil rights movement — is indeed nothing less than an outrage.

Obama, his first attorney general, Eric Holder, and Holder's successor, Loretta Lynch, are three blacks who sold out the black community by equating the civil rights movement with LGBT rights.

Few remember it now, but in his first presidential campaign, Obama voiced support for traditional marriage. As he prepared for reelection, I warned that President Obama was too beholden to LGBT activists and would not keep his promise on marriage.

Just as I had predicted, Obama soon betrayed us on marriage and began a campaign to push the LGBT agenda. Worse still, he tried to equate issues like transgender bathrooms and taxpayer-funded sex changes with the great civil rights movement of the 1960s. Obama helped the LGBT community hijack our civil rights movement.

I publicly criticized Obama for his actions, saying that I had marched with Dr. King for freedom and equality. But not one step that we took was in support of same-sex marriage.

As the efforts to co-opt the mantle of civil rights grew more pronounced, I found myself called upon to speak for the millions of black Americans that stood — and still stand — for Biblical values and Christian principle.

In 2014, I led CAAP's campaign calling for the impeachment of Eric Holder since he had violated his oath of office by attempting to impose same-sex marriage on the nation. The announcement of that campaign came on the same day Holder invited state attorneys general to refuse to defend laws banning same-sex marriage.

I argued that Holder should be impeached because of his repeated lawlessness in trying to impose gay marriage throughout the country. It was one thing for him to make a political argument that gay marriage should be the law, but it was quite another to take actions that ignored the federal Defense of Marriage Act (DOMA), Supreme Court rulings, and the constitutions of dozens of states that specifically rejected the redefinition of marriage.

The Left wants us to forget how same-sex marriage was imposed upon our country in defiance of the clearly expressed will of the people. In-state after-state, Americans voted to restrict marriage to one man and one woman. We believed that our votes had power because we believed that our leaders in Washington would follow the rule of law and heed the voice of the people.

Because of the efforts and determination of our Founding Fathers, we have a government of, by, and for the people. DOMA was passed by the people's representatives in Congress and signed into law. The citizens of the United States and those of states who voted to preserve marriage between a man and woman through amendments to their state constitutions had their votes voided and thrown out by radical federal judges and the Obama administration — particularly the Department of Justice.

Yes, "We the People" voted for members of Congress who passed DOMA, and citizens in 31 states voted to pass constitutional amendments that defined marriage as the union between one man and one woman. But with the support of President Barack Obama and his nomination of liberal judges to federal courts, those votes by "We the

People" were stolen from us. The Supreme Court is not a legislative body and should not overturn the will of people who have voted in the states for a constitutional amendment that bans same-sex marriage.

I believe Holder was so political in his zeal to redefine marriage that he was willing to run roughshod over the rulings of the Supreme Court, binding federal law, and the United States Constitution along with the constitutions of most states. Yet, our leaders in Washington were willing to let him get away with his illegal conduct and did nothing meaningful to hold him accountable.

I also called upon Supreme Court Justices Ruth Bader Ginsburg and Elena Kagan to recuse themselves from the same-sex marriage case of *Obergefell v. Hodges*. Both justices had previously officiated at same-sex weddings in states in which they were legal before the decision in Obergefell. I believed their failure to recuse themselves was a breach of ethics and called into question the integrity of the nation's highest court.

A Supreme Court justice is called upon to avoid the appearance of bias, particularly during a very controversial and sensitive issue that is before the court. Both Justices Ginsburg and Kagan had taken a public stance in favor of same-sex marriage and officiated at these weddings.

In 2015, on the 50th anniversary of the "Bloody Sunday" march in Selma, Alabama — where blacks were beaten while demanding voting rights they were denied — Obama dared to compare this revered event in black history to the agenda for gay marriage.

President Obama was a disgrace to the black community on that day. He attempted to rewrite history. We didn't suffer and die for gay marriage. We marched for opportunity, equality, justice, and freedom from oppression. Blacks are the true heirs of the civil rights movement, and LGBT special interest groups cannot claim it as their own.

The radical LGBT community hijacked our civil rights movement — which they know nothing about. I believe

Obama was delusional to compare our struggle with the campaign for same-sex marriage. Gays have not had fire hoses, or dogs unleashed at them. They have not been hanged from trees or denied basic human rights. It is no less than a disgrace and a lie to say that blacks marched so that gays would have the right to marry today.

When we look at what was behind Obama's support for the LGBT lobby, we see that it really was about politics and paying back special interest groups. Obama once said he believed in traditional marriage, but later announced his position had "evolved." He deceived the American people. Obama made a deal with leaders of the gay community to support him in his re-election bid, assuring them he would take up the gay marriage issue after he had won. Some very wealthy LGBT lobbyists contributed significant amounts to Obama's re-election campaign, and the president made good on the deal.

I marched during the civil rights movement with many people who were as shocked as I was to hear gay and transgender rights being equated with civil rights for blacks. Not one person I have spoken to from back in the days of the civil rights marches has agreed with this comparison.

There is also simply no relation between the struggles that black Americans have faced and the desires of a tiny minority group of individuals of one sex who claim to be the opposite sex. What do the struggles of black Americans to be treated as humans have to do with men who claim to be women invading the dignity and privacy of women and girls in public spaces? Once again, to suggest some equivalence in these ideas is a gross insult to all of us who marched and faced hatred in the name of equality. President Obama's support for legislation that would amend the Civil Rights Act to prohibit discrimination based on sex, sexual orientation, or gender identity is an affront to the black community and theft of the civil rights legacy.

I want to be clear: Transgender persons are not asking for equal rights — they are asking for special rights that violate the privacy of women and girls in public bathrooms and other facilities and defy simple common sense.

We should not allow the gay and transgender community to rob black Americans of their battle for civil rights. I truly believe that if the leaders of the civil rights movement were alive today, they would be angered over the attempt to equate LGBT "rights" with the black civil rights movement in the same way that Jesus was angered when he turned over the tables of the money changers!

Through both its churches and its traditions, black America has shown that we have the moral authority to lead. But we cannot let our moral leadership be bought by large sums of money from the LGBT community. I love everyone that has been created in the image of God, but I refuse to adopt and promote sinful lifestyles that lead to destruction. Christians are called to be royal ambassadors for Christ. Whether we are in our schools, our communities, or the voting booth, we should be ambassadors for Christ. I am.

> I love everyone that has been created in the image of God, but I refuse to adopt and promote sinful lifestyles that lead to destruction

Throughout our nation, we see the destructive effects of the Supreme Court's decision to push same-sex marriage on Americans. One-way religious liberty is being systematically dismantled is by forcing businesses to bow down to the LGBTQ extremists. Christian business owners are being forced to participate in same-sex marriage ceremonies they find repulsive or shut their businesses down. Even Christians, Muslims, and other people of faith are being told they must change their religious beliefs to accommodate the extremists. This is not an exaggeration — it's the kind of promise that is regularly made in political speeches and campaigns when they think Christians aren't paying attention. Hillary Clinton campaigned for the presidency while backing LGBT extremists and saying that religious groups must change to allow for sexual perversion to be normalized.

When Democrats try to understand how Donald Trump defeated Hillary Clinton in 2016, maybe they should read what the Bible says about reaping what you sow.

One of the reasons that Deborah and I have devoted so many years of our lives defending God's plan for marriage is that we wanted to prevent what is going on right now in our culture. Knowing the tactics and ideology of leftists as we do, we tried to sound the alarm when Christians were told not to worry about same-sex marriage because it wouldn't affect them. We knew that was a lie. Not only are our religious liberties being lost, now our children are entering an era of experimentation and manipulation that future generations will look on with horror.

Can you imagine what people will say in the future when they hear that people of our time let children undergo radical sex reassignment medical treatments rather than treating their psychological issues? Let us hope that they won't compare us to Dr. Mengele, the Nazi who performed gruesome experiments on Jewish children during the holocaust.

Now, we have our government telling kindergarten students that they can decide for themselves if they want to be a boy or a girl. We have schools that will single out young men and women who teachers (not trained psychiatrists) think might be questioning their sexual identity. Without informing or involving the parents, the teachers can give those children materials and counseling on gender transition or sexual preference. We now have parents who refuse to let even family members know what sex a child is at birth so that one day, that child can decide for him or herself what sex it wants to be.

This is not just wrongheaded and dangerous; it defies the will of God. God does not make mistakes. As the Bible states, he designed us both male and female. The wickedness of sexual or gender confusion is not coming from God. Paul wrote that God is not a God of confusion but of organization and of a sound mind. All these sexually confusing forces now running rampant through our society were unleashed after the Supreme Court's ruling on same-sex marriage.

Once again, we ask the leftists, "Where does it end? What will you accept as a victory? When will you stop pushing us continually toward destruction?" The answer is that the leftists hate America and will not stop until America is destroyed. Where does black America stand in a destroyed America? We don't stand at all.

As to the child experimentation going on, I don't just wonder about what the future holds. I scream out, "What are you thinking?" How many hours have you devoted to prayer about what you are doing with your children? Black America, why do you vote for Democratic candidates who wittingly or unwittingly support these sexual extremists who think they know — better than you — what is best for your children?

Have you ever wondered what will happen when a boy decides that he wants to be a girl when he is five years old? And then that boy created by God becomes a girl created by man. What happens when your son or grandson falls in love with that "girl" who has God's DNA as a man? Will your son be attracted toward a man or a woman? If they get married, they cannot have children together. Such social experimentation will give a whole new meaning to the 1970s song "Le Freak." Who is going to pay for the artificial hormones that may cost $100,000 a year to keep that God-created-boy looking like a "girl"? The taxpayers? After all, progressives and leftists always want to raise our taxes to pay for everything. It's yet another way that leftists' policies are quickening the fall of America. We cannot even pay for the unsustainable Obamacare. How are we as a nation to pay for all these artificial hormones and sexual surgeries?

As these wicked forces push our society toward social anarchy, there will be false prophets in our churches calling for deviation from biblical principles. The Bible tells us to expect it. When humans gather and determine their moral compass without God, then God help us! The good news is that He will. Pray without ceasing and keep on reading.

Rev. Bill and Deborah Owens Speak at March for Marriage in DC / 2014

9

**OUR BLACK BABIES WILL
CARRY ON OUR
HERITAGE,
SO WHY ARE WE
DESTROYING THEM
THROUGH ABORTION?**

I n August of 2018, Chelsea Clinton, the daughter of Bill and Hillary Clinton, spoke at a pro-abortion event. She claimed that since the legalization of abortion in 1973, abortion had financially helped America by adding 3.5 trillion more dollars to the economy. But she is dead wrong — 58 million dead babies wrong. She came up with that bogus statistic by estimating how many more women entered the workforce. She did not estimate how much our economy was hurt by these 58 million babies not being fed, clothed, educated, and then entering the workforce and paying taxes. The entire Social Security system relies on more workers entering the workforce.

And she didn't calculate the harm that abortion has done to black families. The saddest fact for black Americans is that black babies are aborted at a much higher rate than white babies. Let's look at abortion and black America.

More blacks in America have died from abortion than from all diseases and violent crime combined.[31]

This, to me, is a sobering statement of fact. But sadly, there are more staggering statistics.

More than 19 million black babies have been aborted since 1973 when the Supreme Court created a constitutional right to abortion in Roe v. Wade — though no such right ever existed in the Constitution. Abortion has diminished the black population by more than 25 percent!

The Summary of Vital Statistics 2012: The City of New York reported that more black babies were killed by abortion than were born that year, with 42.4 percent of the total number of abortions in that city performed on black babies.[32]

The Centers for Disease Control and Prevention (CDC) has, even more, to tell us about blacks and abortion.[33]

During the 1970s, about 24 percent of all abortions in America were performed on black women. That percentage jumped to 30 percent during the 1980s and higher still to 34 percent in the 1990s.

Through much of the 2000s, the percentage of abortions performed on black babies held steady at nearly 36 percent, even though blacks represent only about 13 percent of the population.

Today in America, a black baby is three times more likely to be killed in his or her mother's womb than a white baby, and the average black woman is nearly five times more likely to have an abortion than the average white woman.[34]

> Today in America, a black baby is three times more likely to be killed in his or her mother's womb than a white baby

Yes, I am using the word "killed." Planned Parenthood and the rest of the abortion industry — and now Black Lives Matter — call abortion "healthcare" and "reproductive justice," but that is the Left is trying to control the media narrative. They try to sanitize abortion when the truth is that abortion is murder.

Think about it. How many future Martin Luther King's, Coretta Scott King's, Rosa Parks, Mamie Till Mobley's, or black NASA engineers like Dorothy Vaughan, Katherine Johnson, and Mary Jackson have we aborted? Black Lives Matter doesn't want anyone believing black babies in the womb matter. That would defeat its political agenda to incite divisiveness.

A reduction in the black population has been part of the Left's agenda for decades. Planned Parenthood — America's largest abortion provider – was founded by Margaret Sanger, a eugenicist who began the Negro Project in 1939 as an attempt to bring birth control to blacks and reduce their population. The Negro Project was advertised as a remedy to poverty and high birth rates in the black community. Sanger joined with elite African Americans of her era, including Mary McLeod Bethune, W.E.B. DuBois, and Rev. Adam Clayton Powell Sr., to promote her philosophy of reducing the black population. Sanger said that blacks were "unfit," along with other groups, such as the disabled.

Sanger wrote in *The Pivot of Civilization*:[35]

> Everywhere we see poverty and large families going hand in hand. Those least fit to carry on the race are increasing most rapidly. People who cannot support their own offspring are encouraged by Church and State to produce large families. Many of the children, thus begotten, are diseased or feeble-minded; many become criminals. The burden of supporting these unwanted types must be borne by the healthy elements of the nation. Funds that should be used to raise the standard of our civilization are diverted to the maintenance of those who should never have been born.

In 1937, Sanger and her colleagues drafted a report on "Birth Control and the Negro" that stated, "[N]egroes present the great problem of the South," because they have, "the greatest economic, health and social problems." The report portrayed blacks as illiterates who, "still breed carelessly and disastrously."[36]

Sanger's condescension toward blacks was obvious as she contrived ways to get blacks to buy into her goal of reducing their population.

In a 1939 letter[37] to physician and philanthropist Charles Gamble, who was also seeking massive birth control use for those he deemed uneducated, Sanger wrote:

> It seems to me in my experience where I have been in North Carolina, Georgia, Tennessee, and Texas, that while the colored Negroes have great respect for white doctors they can get closer to their own members and more or less lay their cards on the table which means their ignorance, superstitions, and doubts.

Sanger also knew blacks were strongly influenced by the Church and decided the best way to sell birth control to them was through their pastors. In the same letter to Gamble, she wrote:

> The ministers work is also important and, he should be trained, perhaps by the Federation as to our ideals and the goal we hope to reach. We do not want word to go out that we want to exterminate the Negro population and the minister is the man who can straighten out that idea if it ever occurs to any of their more rebellious members.

Sanger even addressed women who were members of the Ku Klux Klan in New Jersey in 1926.

Today, Planned Parenthood has an abortion facility in New York City named after its founder, Margaret Sanger. And the presidential candidate Planned Parenthood endorsed in the 2016 election was Hillary Clinton. Clinton was prepared to promote even more abortions and to repeal the Hyde Amendment, which bars taxpayer funds from being used for abortions. She wanted even more minority women to have access to abortion.

"I admire Margaret Sanger enormously," Clinton said in 2009 when she accepted Planned Parenthood's Margaret Sanger award. "Her courage, her tenacity, her vision."[38]

"When I think about what [Sanger] did all those years ago in Brooklyn," Clinton continued, "I am really in awe of her. And there are a lot of lessons that we can learn from her life and the cause she launched and fought for and sacrificed so greatly."

Today, Planned Parenthood performs over 320,000 abortions per year and takes in more than $500 million in taxpayer funds. This "nonprofit" does make a profit on abortions, however. In its 2016-2017 annual report, Planned

Parenthood's profits rose by $21 million — or 27 percent — from the year before.[39]

Perhaps it is not ironic at all that as the number of abortions has decreased in the United States, the number performed at Planned Parenthood has persistently increased, as has its market share percentage of total abortion procedures.[40]

Planned Parenthood is a finely-tuned abortion business that has captured 35 percent of the U.S. abortion market — well above the market shares of leaders of other major U.S. industries.[41] About 80 percent of Planned Parenthood's surgical abortion facilities are located within walking distance of black or Hispanic neighborhoods. (*For more data, see Appendix B, Abortion.*)

This is a major reason why I am encouraging blacks to educate themselves about the Democratic Party. While our babies are being aborted, Planned Parenthood is donating millions of dollars to the Democrats because they know that with Democrats in power, they will get even more taxpayer funding and continue to get coverage as "healthcare providers" when they are really running abortion mills.

Sadly, though Republicans claim to be the "pro-life" party, even with control of Congress and the White House, they did not fully defund Planned Parenthood.

These are indeed sobering statistics. But there is light in the darkness. Working to defeat abortion helps you meet some of the most courageous and faith-filled people in this country. What's more, seeing the harm that flows from the Culture of Death that surrounds abortion brings you more awareness of the blessings of life, all life, and how there is dignity in every human being.

I'm sure that some of you have known about this holocaust of unborn black infants for years. But some of you have never heard about how our black babies are being killed at rates that are staggering compared to lynching and murders that are sewn through our history. How can we stop the shootings in our inner cities when we have no respect for the life of our youngest and most vulnerable black citizens being nourished in their mothers' wombs?

The leftist agenda has purposely deceived us. They want us to look away from our dying black babies. Instead, we are told to be angry toward the white Founders. We are told to blame Republicans for everything. We are taught not to be thankful for America but to hate it until it is destroyed. I must ask this question: what happens if the leftists take over all positions of power one day? Will black America be free then?

> The truth is that the progressive Left's message to black America is only about keeping or gaining power

The truth is that the progressive Left's message to black America is only about keeping or gaining power. And power games can easily be seen for what they are. For a startling example of the Left's tendency to reduce politics to power, look no further than what happened after President Trump won the 2016 election. Trump Derangement Syndrome became a virus, infecting Hillary voters and establishment politicians alike. The thought of losing power causes human beings to act differently. Reason goes by the wayside, and some indulge in the worst tendencies of human nature — vindictiveness, immaturity, and a desire to destroy their "enemy," even if it means violating every standard of decency and principle.

Look around you. If blacks begin to vote for the candidates and party most closely aligned with biblical principles, who loses? Black America has been losing for 50 years now. If most black citizens started voting Biblical values, then the only black Americans who will lose are those who guarantee so many votes for the Democratic Party each election.

Let me be blunt. Black leaders looking for brown paper bags with "money sandwiches" and "gas money" might lose something on Election Day. But if you have not been receiving "gas money" or financial perks for voting in the past for Democratic candidates, then you have nothing to lose. Try voting your values and your conscience and see if the Democratic Party will go back to biblical values. If enough blacks vote their core values, then blacks in America may take up President Trump's mantra — we will start winning so much that we will get tired of winning.

Let's try it. What do we have to lose? Maybe we will lose the chaos and drugs of our inner cities. Maybe we will lose our failing school systems. Maybe we will lose our dependency on the broken welfare system that keeps our mothers single and our children fatherless. Maybe our overcrowded prisons can be emptied, and the Ten Commandments can be respected once again. Put those thoughts on your prayer list and pray about what God is calling you to do.

A Poem on Abortion by William Owens, Jr. *The Melody of My Life*

10

HOW BLACK AMERICANS CAN RISE FROM THE LIES OF THE LEFT

shared with you my life transformation in December 1988 when, after much despair, I heard God's call and put His plan for me into action by helping black Americans get a college education. Through my work with Give Me a Chance Ministry, I believe I was helping my brothers and sisters rise from government dependence to a life of dignity and pride. I want all blacks to experience this so that our people can finally cross the Jordan and reach the Promised Land!

In these pages, I have tried to show you how the lies of the Left and its ideology have gotten our people stuck in the quagmire of government dependence, destroying our families and weakening our culture. By bowing to liberals in government, our rightful place as heirs to the civil rights movement has been usurped by the radical LGBT lobby and even by individuals who have come to our country illegally. Democratic politicians — voted into office by most blacks — fund their campaigns with money from Planned Parenthood, an organization that has, through abortion, made a black mother's womb the most dangerous place for our babies.

Dr. King would say, "Whenever men and women straighten their backs up, they are going somewhere, because a man can't ride your back unless it is bent."

I refuse to believe that we have lost our ability to recognize the wisdom in this statement. Young children are taught about the civil rights movement in grade school. Dr. King's essays and speeches are studied and repeated over and over. But his message of dignity through self-reliance has been obscured by the effort to keep black Americans subservient.

We have too many black backs bent with government hand-outs riding them down. But it doesn't have to be this way. Blacks have attached themselves to the Democratic Party and its leadership. But that Party wants votes more than it wants free black men and women who are financially

> It is time to stop voting for candidates who take our vote for granted!

independent. For over 50 years, blacks in America have pledged their allegiance to the Democratic Party. It is time to stop voting for candidates who take our vote for granted! It is past time to stop listening to their rhetoric!

Left-wing movements like climate change and political correctness are nothing more than power moves to gain more control over individuals. Yes, I want clean air and water, but we do not have to listen to a liberal press that has convinced blacks that our cities on the coasts will be underwater without drastic action. Listen to scientists on both sides of the issue. Let's stop being ignorant! Turn off CNN and MSNBC and read or watch news that provides a perspective different from the liberal talking points! Fair and balanced news is not what black America has heard for the most part.

In recent months, I have found myself the unexpected spokesperson for African Americans who are tired of seeing race used to divide and politically manipulate our people. It started when I criticized Nike and athlete-turned-activist Colin Kaepernick for leftist, anti-American politics. The company had pulled a shoe celebrating the Betsy Ross flag based on criticism from Kaepernick. Though I later wrote an open letter to Kaepernick, inviting him to find more practical ways to help African Americans, I couldn't allow the denigration of such an important American symbol go unchecked. CAAP called on Nike to sever its relationship with Kaepernick. As I explained, this kind of misguided thinking attempts to erase American history, belittles the African American experience, and sets the wrong example for young people.

Because I would not bow to the Left's attempt to redefine racism, I found myself the target of attacks. It culminated in a CNN appearance wherein host Don Lemon attempted to get me to say that President Donald Trump is racist. As I had just come from a White House meeting where the president sought out black pastors and leaders in the attempt to address African American concerns, I didn't agree with Lemon and the Left's attempt to smear the president with that term. Because I wouldn't toe the leftist line, Lemon attempted to attack me instead. On Twitter afterward, some people called the performance, "journalistic malpractice." I admit that I had to laugh when I learned that they had identified me as a "pastor" for the first part of the interview, but when I wouldn't follow their lead, I became a "controversial pastor."

Why do I persist in arguing against outrage culture and the tendency to use the term "racism" as a political weapon? Because this is not a tactic that will help black Americans get to the Promised Land. It is mere manipulation, a strategy that will keep us focused on our grievances rather than the ways that we can leverage our gifts and influence to improve our people.

We must educate ourselves because the elitists who control the press want to silence any science that does not prop up their ideology. Think about this for a moment. With our scientific technology, mothers can see an ultrasound of their unborn babies with all their human parts. But Planned Parenthood and the rest of the abortion industry fight state laws that require a woman to have an ultrasound before an abortion. Why? Because they know most women and girls would question their decision to abort their babies if they saw that ultrasound of a live baby, not just a "clump of cells" (as they like to call an unborn baby). The abortion lobby and their friends in the media would rather prevent a woman from seeing the whole truth — via science — to meet their own end — more profits from abortion. Yet, they claim conservatives are anti-science!

What blacks in America need now more than ever is complete independence from the government and left-wing ideology. That will never happen with the Democratic Party controlling the black vote.

So how do we shake off the lies of the Left and rise to claim that Promised Land, "flowing with milk and honey?"

Let's consider these ten ways:

1. End Racism

The first major step may be controversial, but after a lifetime of experience, I believe this will help us break through the mystical barrier that has managed to keep us from the Promised Land. We need to stop using the word "racism." The very word itself divides us. The word "racism" declares that we are separate races. If we are one race, which God in the Bible says we are, there cannot be racism.

Don't get me wrong. I have experienced pain, separation, and discrimination because of the color of my skin. But racism is nothing more than a common sin experienced by every society — the sin of favoritism. Just as the early church was chastised for showing the sin of favoritism, so too our society falls into error and engages in favoritism as well. I proclaim that if we are true to God's word, then we are one race — the human race. If we show favoritism to those like ourselves, then we are guilty of favoritism. We can defeat racism by defeating the sin of favoritism and uniting as the brothers and sisters that we are.

> If we show favoritism to those like ourselves, then we are guilty of favoritism

If we use the term "racism," then we are committed to the belief that we are more than one race. That rewards those who are working to divide us for their purposes — including the master of deception, the devil himself!

Think about the freedom that we experience when we rid ourselves of racial thinking. In *Up From Slavery*, Booker T. Washington wrote that "With God's help, I believe I have completely rid myself of any ill-feeling toward the Southern white man for any wrong that he may have inflicted upon my race."

Washington continued by saying that he pitied, "any individual who is so unfortunate as to get into the habit of holding race prejudice."

CAAP has launched a new initiative called RISE[42], an exclusive grassroots network uniting people of every race, creed, culture, and background. We created RISE specifically to show that favoritism has no part in the fight to save our country. When we share the same values and principles, everything else disappears — leaving only a powerful force for faith, family, and freedom.

Visit the website www.caapusa.org to find out more about RISE.

2. Go Back to Biblical Values

Dr. Martin Luther King, Jr. once preached a sermon[43] that said we must go back before we can go forward. We must go back to the Bible to rediscover our lost values. To illustrate his point, he used the image of Jesus as a child being left unknowingly at the temple by his parents, Joseph and Mary. They thought that Jesus was with relatives, and when they discovered he was missing, they had to go back to Jerusalem and find him. Dr. King was telling us through his sermon that, yes, we must go back to the Bible to find Jesus.

As we go back, we must rediscover the Ten Commandments (there's a good reason why ten is one of my favorite numbers) which the Founders of our great nation used in creating our philosophy of government. Communities that strive to promote and live by the Ten Commandments that Moses brought down from Mount Sinai are communities that thrive.

The Ten Commandments are beautiful in the way they layout, simply and clearly, the rules by which one should live. Imagine a country where the Ten Commandments were the way of judging right. Imagine how the Commandments could sweep away the lies of relativism and modernism that have polluted modern morality. We must go back to these time-tested, biblical, Judeo-Christian values that our nation was founded! We should strive to place the Ten Commandments in our schools, our communities and on our streets! Be blessed, live out God's Ten Commandments.

3. Build Businesses Everywhere

What black communities need now more than ever are entrepreneurs. However, years of increased regulation and taxes discouraged entrepreneurship, leading to a negative trend in new businesses that are only beginning to correct itself under Trump.[44] For "a people" who are seeking to achieve self-reliance and enter the Promised Land, opportunity is essential. For black Americans to achieve financial independence, we need to be a nation of entrepreneurs.

Under the Obama administration, government regulations and mandates grew enormously, choking out the new businesses that account for most new jobs. Today, as I write this, the Trump administration is cutting government regulations and bringing back jobs — the highest number of jobs that black Americans have been able to attain in years! As I noted earlier, we are living in an unprecedented time. We can contrast how the economy did under the leftist policies of our first black president with the first months of President Trump's policies. Vote accordingly. Never forget that those new jobs are the route to financial independence — if only we would reach out and grab it!

If you're a young black person, now is your time to shine as an entrepreneur. It would be good to acknowledge that this is because of the policies enacted by President Trump.

4. Embrace New Technology

Even though I believe we must go back to Biblical values, I am not afraid for entrepreneurs to brainstorm and be a part of the new technological revolution. Though I am a bit of a novice when it comes to the internet, I use cell phones. I use the technology that makes it easier for me to communicate and makes my days more productive.

If I can learn how to take advantage of these advances, anyone can. That's why I encourage black Americans to be a part of technological innovations. How will our black businesses grow and thrive unless they offer what is best for everyone — not just the black community? Black Americans have been gifted with unique insights by virtue of their experiences — insights into dealing with people who may look different than we are and insights in building relationships across cultural divides. With these insights and innovative new technology, black entrepreneurs can build dreams that the whole world will marvel. Start building!

5. Education

We must ensure that black America experiences a revolution in education, raising the achievement of all black children. The culture of black America has not always rewarded education or placed the necessary value on education, either throughout our communities or throughout our lifetimes. Never has technology offered so much potential to leapfrog the field of education. Black America should lead the way.

> Black America should lead the way

My wife, Deborah, and I have dedicated our lives to education. We know first-hand how education changes lives and paves the way for those who seek it constantly. What we want is to inspire the desire to seek knowledge and wisdom.

The Bible says that as a child, Jesus grew in stature with both God and man. We want black America to embrace that model through education in how God made this world (math, science, literature, history, etc.) and in how to better understand God (Bible study).

6. Politics

We live in a constitutional republic. For the past 50 years, our so-called black leaders have bought into a system based on the theory that if black Americans vote as a block, it will bring us more power and influence. I am telling you today that their theory has failed! Look at our cities! Look at our prisons! Look at our lines for government help!

Do we really have a dominant voice? Yes, we helped elect Barack Obama, and then we helped re-elect him. But did conditions for black America change significantly during those eight years? The black vote has empowered a few blacks to be nothing more than the equivalent of the "money-changers" in the temple before Jesus took a whip and ran them out. It's time for black America to do the same.

Our politicians in the Congressional Black Caucus are way past their prime — it's time for a sweeping change! Vote for candidates and not political parties! The Democratic Party's stranglehold on the black vote needs to end now. The socialists and radical leftists are taking over the Democratic Party. Where will you stand? We have nothing to lose and the Promised Land to gain!

7. Work for Peace

Dr. King's great legacy is deeper than his contribution to racial equality in America (as important as that is). His impact is global because his message was global. Dr. King and other civil rights leaders stood for justice and peace, concepts that don't have boundaries. They taught by example, showing us how to work for peace in the world. Moreover, they showed us that our mission should extend anywhere that injustice exists. As black Americans transform their lives in working together to cross into the Promised Land, we cannot forget — nor can we neglect — those souls around the world who need hope.

We all need hope. Black America needs hope. That is exactly why I am writing this book. When I sat in my mother's house, praying for guidance in that long-ago December, I was in despair. But it was when all my hope was gone that I received a divine gift. God spoke to me in my spirit, as He seeks to speak to everyone on this earth. Therefore, as we work together, we must work for peace and meet the challenges of this changing world. Like Dr. King and other leaders in the civil rights movement, we do so by leading by example. We can teach how hope springs eternal as we sing the song for freedom right here in America.

When I was writing this book in the summer of 2018, I was invited to meet with a group of African American pastors at the White House on the issue of prison reform. I felt that we had a productive meeting, and the president wanted to hear our input. But when the news of the meeting reached the public, I was not prepared for the words leveled by so-called black leaders at other pastors and me. I was shocked. How could I be the target of so much invective when my only crime was seeking to help those in prison … and being willing to discuss the matter with the President of the United States?

My first human reaction was anger. But I thought about my mother. I thought about Dr. King and his "Letter from Birmingham Jail." I wanted to lash out at those who verbally abused me for meeting with President Trump. But mother taught me to love, even in difficult circumstances. So, I reached out to those who wanted to persecute me with an open letter. We may not agree on everything, but we must love each other and build each other up for black America to get to the Promised Land. We will not get there one by one; we must cross the Jordan River together.

The children of Israel crossed the Jordan River as God blocked the waters from flowing. Could this time of economic prosperity be the window of opportunity black America needs to cross the river to the Promised Land?

8.   Life

My wife and I are pro-life. My good friend, Dr. Alveda King, has worked with us and helped us learn more about the damage abortion has done to the black community. Dr. Alveda King is the niece of Dr. Martin Luther King, Jr., and she has helped lead the way for the civil rights of the unborn. Unfortunately, black America still needs to come to terms with what is happening to our people because of abortion.

For black America to achieve all we can be, we must once again make sure that unborn black babies are safe from the death and destruction of abortion. The liberal Democrats who say they love black Americans must prove it by ending abortion-on-demand in our communities. They must prove it by shutting down the abortion services of Planned Parenthood and ending the deception that abortion is a necessity for black women and girls. When we show respect for life in the womb, it will flow outward through our culture, increasing respect for life across the board. And if we can increase respect for the sanctity of human life, I believe we will see the tragic murder rate of black-on-black crime go down dramatically.

9.   Crime

We need prison reform and prisoner rehabilitation. But prison reform should not start with the government releasing potentially still-dangerous criminals back into our neighborhoods. Prison reform should start with our churches and our communities. It starts with going back to teaching the Ten Commandments. We need them in our churches, in our schools (both public and private), and on our courthouse squares.

Crime is taking over our streets, killing our people, and destroying our sense of community. Black Americans live in fear, whether on the streets of Chicago or in Memphis. Therefore, I say to place the Ten Commandments on your tee shirts, on your hats, and everywhere we can put them. Take them to the streets. Demand the right to place the Ten Commandments in public places. If your candidates for public office will not stand up for the Ten Commandments, tell them to forget your vote. God's laws provide thousands of years worth of wisdom on how to live life successfully and be blessed. Crime cannot thrive in communities that respect the Ten Commandments.

10. Stand for Israel

In Genesis, God tells us He will bless those who stand with His chosen people. Some people say that it does not apply today. Since when does God say something He does not mean? If we, as a people, want to get to the Promised Land, then we, as a people, need to help those who made it to the Promised Land.

Dr. King had many Jewish friends and donors. He went to Israel and told of that experience in his speeches. The success of the civil rights movement would not have happened without our Jewish friends. We have friends in Israel, and we need to stand by them. The more we study God's Word, the closer we get to God and the closer we get to the Promised Land.

I love America. It is the greatest country in the world. I have had many sorrows, but the joys have outweighed the pain and suffering. I have fulfilled many of my dreams, and I am still dreaming and overcoming. The lessons I learned from my mother and other mentors, I have passed on to my children and grandchildren. They are now dreaming bigger dreams and are themselves, great achievers. Where else in the world can this happen but in America? America allows one the freedom to dream. The freedom to achieve. That is the America I love.

> America allows one the freedom to dream. The freedom to achieve. That is the America I love.

In our America, I love, the black community is poised to transform itself. I am convinced that God will give us His guidance as we make this transformation. The visitation from God I received in 1988 transformed my life in ways I could not anticipate or engineer. In the end, it was God's grace that demonstrated to me that, "all things are possible." It was by the grace of God that He poured out His grace in my life in an unexpected way.

Deborah and I pray that you, too, will be inspired by this book to open your heart to God's grace. May it deepen your understanding of what blacks need to do to accept God's outpouring of grace. I mentioned earlier that I have always liked the number ten. As a young activist, I saw how the ten commandments formulated by Dr. King as the foundation of his non-violent approach won freedom for blacks in America. You can see how much I believe in God's Ten Commandments. And now you have read about my ten action items — the strategies I believe will propel black America into the Promised Land.

May my words enlighten you, allowing you to dream God-inspired dreams, quicken you to action, and provide a hope that never fails. May God bless you and keep you. The Lord make His face shine upon you, And be gracious to you; The Lord lift His countenance upon you.

And may God spark our transformation as a people who will finally reach the Promised Land!

A message
for black
voters

Appendix A - Useful Charts and Graphs

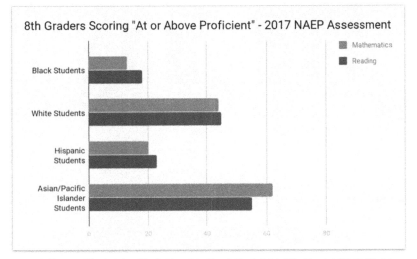

8th Graders Scoring "At or Above Proficient" - 2017 NAEP Assessment

Source: U.S. Department of Education, Institute of Education Sciences, National Center for Education Statistics, National Assessment of Educational Progress (NAEP), 2017 Mathematics Assessment.

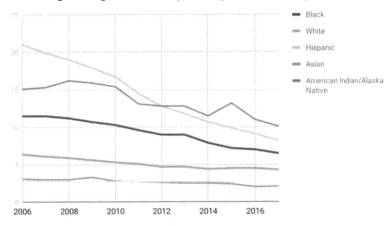

Percentage of High School Dropouts, by Race/Ethnicity

Source: U.S. Department of Commerce, Census Bureau, American Community Survey (ACS), 2006 through 2017.

Students Receiving Expulsions, by Race/Ethnicity

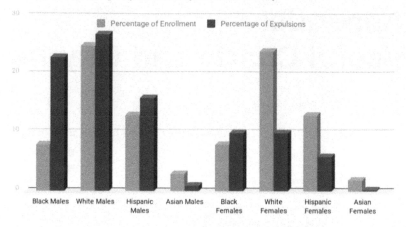

Source: U.S. Department of Education, Office for Civil Rights, Civil Rights Data Collection, 2015-2016.

Imprisonment Rates of Sentenced State & Federal Prisoners per 100,000 U.S. Residents of Corresponding Race/Origin, Dec. 31, 2017

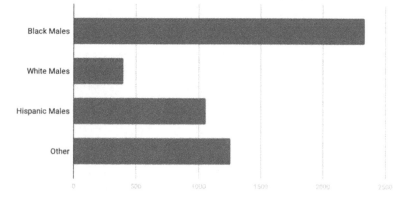

Source: U.S. Department of Justice, Bureau of Justice Statistics, Prisoners in 2017

Reported Abortions by Race/Ethnicity, Selected Reporting Areas, United States - 2015

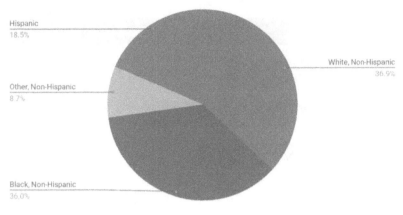

Hispanic
18.5%

White, Non-Hispanic
36.9%

Other, Non-Hispanic
8.7%

Black, Non-Hispanic
36.0%

Source: Centers for Disease Control

Abortions by Race/Ethnicity per 1000 Women in Same Racial/Ethnic Group, 2015

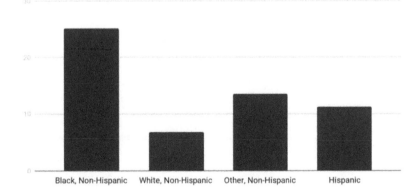

Source: Centers for Disease Control

Abortion Ratio (Number of abortions by race/ethnicity per 1000 live births to women in same racial/ethnic group), 2015

Source: Centers for Disease Control

Appendix B - Just the Facts

General
- In the U.S. House, only 63 percent of the 244 Democrats who voted on the Civil Rights Act approved it, while 80 percent of the 171 Republicans voted in favor of it. In the Senate, the final tally was 73 in favor and 23 against the act. Of the 67 Democrats, 69 percent approved it, while 27 of the 33 Republicans, or 82 percent, voted in favor of the Civil Rights Act.
- In only four years, the Give Me a Chance ministry was able to increase the black enrollment at Oral Roberts University from 5 percent to 22.5 percent.

Education
- Test scores released in 2018 from the National Assessment of Educational Progress (NAEP) – also known as the Nation's Report Card – show that 65 percent of the eighth-graders in American public schools in 2017 were not proficient in reading, and 67 percent were not proficient in mathematics. The NAEP test results are even worse for students in some inner-city school districts – mostly black and Hispanic children.
- The city of Detroit, Michigan, had the lowest percentage of students who scored at the proficient level or higher in both mathematics and reading. Test results from that city saw only 5 percent of eighth-graders proficient or higher in math and only 7 percent performing similarly in reading.
- In Cleveland, Ohio, only 11 percent of students in eighth grade were at proficiency level or higher in math, and only 10 percent reached proficiency level in reading.
- Only 11 percent of eighth-graders in Baltimore, Maryland public schools were proficient or higher in math and only 14 percent in reading.

- The 2018 NAEP test results showed that, in general, higher-performing fourth-grade students remained relatively flat on both mathematics and reading, but lower-performing students declined even further. Thus, students from lower socio-economic groups, including many black children, dropped in their overall test scores, leaving a much wider achievement gap between white and black students.

- According to the Progress in International Reading Literacy Study, United States fourth graders dropped from fifth in the international rankings in 2011 to 13th in 2016 out of 58 international education systems.

- According to the 2017 NAEP, black students in grade 8 had the highest percentage of students scoring "below basic" in mathematics at 53 percent. Only 13 percent of black eighth-graders scored "at or above proficient" (compared to 44 percent of white students, 20 percent of Hispanic students, and 62 percent of Asian/Pacific Islanders). Source: U.S. Department of Education, Institute of Education Sciences, National Center for Education Statistics, National Assessment of Educational Progress (NAEP), 2017 Mathematics Assessment. Available at: https://www.nationsreportcard.gov/ndecore/xplore/NDE

- According to the 2017 NAEP, black students in grade 8 had the highest percentage of students scoring "below basic" in reading at 40 percent. Only 18 percent of black eighth-graders scored "at or above proficient" (compared to 45 percent of white students, 23 percent of Hispanic students, and 55 percent of Asian/Pacific Islanders). Source: U.S. Department of Education, Institute of Education Sciences, National Center for Education Statistics, National Assessment of Educational Progress (NAEP), 2017 Reading Assessment. Available at: https://www.nationsreportcard.gov/ndecore/xplore/NDE

- The status dropout rate (the percentage of 16 to 24-year-olds who are not enrolled in school and have not earned a high school credential, i.e., diploma or G.E.D.) for black Americans was 6.5 percent in 2017. This is the third-highest rate by ethnicity or race but represents a decline from a rate of 11.5 percent in 2006. Source: U.S. Department of Commerce, Census Bureau, American Community Survey (ACS), 2006 through 2017.

- The status dropout rate is higher for black males (8.0 percent) than for black females (4.9 percent). Source: U.S. Department of Commerce, Census Bureau, American Community Survey (ACS), 2006 through 2017.

- Black students are subject to proportionately higher rates of discipline during their schooling years. In 2015-2016, 2.7 million K-12 students received out-of-school suspensions. Though they represent only 8 percent of student enrollment, black students represented 25 percent of male out-of-school suspensions and 14 percent of female out-of-school suspensions. Source: U.S. Department of Education, Office for Civil Rights, Civil Rights Data Collection, 2015-2016. Available at https://www2.ed.gov/about/offices/list/ocr/docs/school-climate-and-safety.pdf

- In 2015-2016, approximately 120,800 students were expelled (about 0.2 percent of total students enrolled). Black students had the highest rates of expulsion relative to enrollment. Though only 8 percent of student enrollment, blacks represented 23 percent of male expulsions and 10 percent of female expulsions. Source: U.S. Department of Education, Office for Civil Rights, Civil Rights Data Collection, 2015-2016. Available at https://www2.ed.gov/about/offices/list/ocr/docs/school-climate-and-safety.pdf

Home/Family

- The median annual household income for a black family in 2017 was $40,232 compared to the national average of $57,652. Source: U.S. Census Bureau, 2017 American Community Survey 1-Year Estimates. Available at: https://factfinder.census.gov/-faces/tableservices/jsf/pages/productview.xhtml?src=bkmk#

- The poverty rate for married black couples with children under 18 is 9.1 percent. The poverty rate for black females with no husband present and children under 18 is 40.5 percent. Source: U.S. Census Bureau, 2017 American Community Survey 1-Year Estimates. Available at: https://factfinder.census.gov/faces/-tableservices/jsf/pages/productview.xhtml?src=bkmk#

- Black Americans are more likely to be Christian than any other ethnicity or race. According to Pew Research Center,

79 percent of blacks identify as Christian (53 percent of whom are "historically black protestants") compared to 77 percent of Hispanics and 70 percent of whites. Source: Pew Research Center, Religious Landscape Study, conducted June 4 to Sept. 30, 2014. Available at https://www.pewresearch.org/fact-tank/2018/04/23/black-americans-are-more-likely-than-overall-public-to-be-christian-protestant/.

- In 2017, the imprisoned rate for sentenced black males was 2336 per 100,000 black male U.S. residents - nearly six times the rate of sentenced white males (397 per 100,000 while male U.S. residents). Source: U.S. Department of Justice, Bureau of Justice Statistics, Prisoners in 2017. Available at https://www.bjs.gov/content/pub/pdf/p17.pdf

Labor/Business

- The Bureau of Labor Statistics reported that the May 2018 unemployment rate for blacks aged 16 and over was 5.9 percent, the lowest it has been since the government started collecting such data in 1972 (46 years ago).
- As of July 2019, the unemployment rate for blacks was 6.0 percent. In March 2010 it was 16.8 percent. Source: U.S Department of Labor, Bureau of Labor Statistics. Available at: https://data.bls.gov/timeseries/LNS14000006
- As of 2012, there were 2.6 million black or African American-owned businesses — an increase of 34 percent from 2012. Source: 2012 Survey of Business Owners, U.S. Census Bureau. Available at: https://www.mbda.gov/sites/mbda.gov/files/migrated/files-attachments/SBO_Facts_BOB.pdf

Government Assistance

- Approximately half of eligible Americans were enrolled in the food stamp program in 2003. However, in 2013, 75 percent of those eligible signed up. By that year, a record 47.6 million Americans were relying on food stamps.
- Data from the U.S. Department of Agriculture shows that in February 2017 — one month after Donald Trump was inaugurated — food stamp enrollment was at 42.3 million. By May 2018, however, participation in the food stamp program dropped to 40 million. More than two million people

got off the food stamp rolls in a little more than a year under Trump.

- In 2013, blacks made up 17.7 percent of those receiving food assistance (not including SNAP, WIC, or reduced/free school meals), 22.8 percent of those receiving transportation assistance, 17.9 percent of those receiving clothing assistance, and 28.5 percent of those receiving housing assistance (not including public housing or housing vouchers). Source: U.S. Census Bureau, Survey of Income and Program Participation, Wave 1, 2014 Panel. Available at: https://www.census.gov/content/-dam/Census/library/publications/2017/demo/p70br-149.pdf
- Approximately 25.1 percent of black households receive food stamp/SNAP benefits. Source: U.S. Census Bureau, 2017 American Community Survey 1-Year Estimates. Available at: https://factfinder.census.gov/faces/tableservices/jsf/pages/productview.xhtml?src=bkmk#
- In the fiscal year 2016, blacks made up 29.1 percent of TANF (Temporary Assistance for Needy Families) recipients. Source: Department of Health and Human Services, National TANF Data File as of 6/26/2017. Available at: https://www.acf.hhs.gov/sites/-default/files/ofa/fy16_characteristics.pdf
- According to the U.S. Census Bureau, blacks are more likely to participate in government assistance programs in a given month, with a participation rate of 41.6 percent in 2012. (Followed by Hispanics at 36.4 percent, Asian/Pacific Islanders at 17.8 percent, and whites at 13.2 percent.) Source: U.S. Census Bureau, *Dynamics of Economic Well-Being: Participation in Government Programs, 2009–2012: Who Gets Assistance?* (May 28, 2015). Available at https://www.census.gov/library/publications/2015/demo/p70-141.html
- Blacks are also more likely to be longer-term participants in government assistance programs (defined as 37-48 months of accumulated participation between 2009 and 2012) with 56.3 percent of blacks being longer-term participants versus 47.2 percent for Asian/Pacific Islanders and 36.9 percent for whites. Source: U.S. Census Bureau, *Dynamics of Economic Well-Being: Participation in Government Programs,*

2009–2012: Who Gets Assistance? (May 28, 2015). Available at https://www.census.gov/library/publications/2015/demo/p70-141.html

Abortion

- More than 19 million black babies have been aborted since 1973, the year *Roe v. Wade* was decided. Abortion has diminished the black population by more than 25 percent.

- More blacks in America have died from abortion than from all diseases and violent crime combined.

- *The Summary of Vital Statistics 2012: The City of New York* reported that more black babies were killed by abortion than were born that year, with 42.4 percent of the total number of abortions in that city performed on black babies.

- According to the Centers for Disease Control (CDC), during the 1970s, about 24 percent of all abortions in America were performed on black women. That percentage jumped to 30 percent during the 1980s and higher still to 34 percent in the 1990s.

- The CDC reports that through much of the 2000s, the percentage of abortions performed on black babies held steady at nearly 36 percent, even though blacks represent only about 13 percent of the population.

- Today in America, a black baby is three times more likely to be killed in his or her mother's womb than a white baby. The average black woman is nearly five times more likely to have an abortion than the average white woman.

- Planned Parenthood performs over 320,000 abortions per year and takes in more than $500 million in taxpayer funds. In its 2016-2017 annual report, Planned Parenthood's profits rose by $21 million – or 27 percent – from the year before.

- Planned Parenthood has captured 35 percent of the U.S. abortion market – well above the market shares of leaders of other major U.S. industries.

- About 80 percent of Planned Parenthood's surgical abortion facilities are located within walking distance of black or Hispanic neighborhoods.

- A 2016 study published in the Open Journal of Preventive Medicine calculated that when abortion is considered among all causes of death, it becomes the leading cause of death by far, with 1.152 million deaths in 2009. This far surpasses heart disease at 599,413 deaths and cancer at 567,628 deaths. For African Americans, induced abortion represented 61.1 percent of deaths compared to 16.4 percent of white deaths. Source: James Studnicki, et al., "Induced Abortion, Mortality, and the Conduct of Science." *Open Journal of Preventive Medicine.* (June 2016). Available at: https://www.scirp.org/journal/-PaperInformation.aspx?paperID=67433

- In 2015, black women had the highest abortion rate at 25.1 per 1000 women (compared to 6.8 abortions per 1000 white women). Black women also have the highest ratio of abortions, 390 abortions per 1000 live births. Source: Centers for Disease Control. Available at https://www.cdc.gov/mmwr/volumes/67/ss/ss6713a1.htm

- When marital status is recorded, the vast majority of abortions performed on black women occur on unmarried women (91.8 percent versus 8.2 percent for married women). Source: Centers for Disease Control. Available at https://www.cdc.gov/mmwr/volumes/67/ss/ss6713a1.htm

- The high abortion rate among black women has had a profound effect on the African American population. In 2009, Michael Novak calculated that "of the 47 million children aborted since 1973, some 16 million have been black. If those children had been allowed to live, the black population would today be about 50 percent larger than it is — about 49 million blacks instead of 33 million. Think of the talents that have been lost. Think about the lost contributions to their own families and the nation." Source: Michael Novak, "Notre Dame Disgrace." National Review (April 9, 2009). Available at: https://www.nationalreview.com/2009/04/notre-dame-disgrace-michael-novak/

Endorsements

Pastor Bill Owens, his wife Deborah, and their two beautiful children have become such a special gift to us. It is their strong faith based on the Judeo-Christian values that founded this great country that binds a black family and a white family in the true meaning of God's love.

This book is a personal and powerful look at history through the eyes of a black American pastor who understands that only Christian values will restore freedom — not only for his people but all people of this great country.

Ralph and Linda Schmidt
Advisory Board Members of CAAP

Rev. Owens represents America's best. Like deep roots of mighty trees that stabilize during storms, his lifetime of experiences anchors his vision in an America today that seems to be tearing itself apart. I believe this book is meant "for such a time as this." Born and raised in poverty during segregation in the South, his ability to overcome the systemic barriers of state-supported institutional racism provides him a voice unlike any other in America.

Throughout his life, advancing education for himself (as well as others) and seeking to serve his Lord and Savior have delivered to him the ability to overcome challenges and obstacles. He has marched for civil rights with Dr. Martin Luther King, Jr. He continues to be driven by scripture: "So if the Son sets you free, you will be free indeed."

Rev. Owens has a robust admiration for those who have paved the way for freedom. He honors those who have sacrificed their lives for freedom, whether they died on the battlefield or in the struggles against slavery and segregation. Rev. Owens lives his life according to the scripture in Hebrews, which says, "Some died by stoning, some were sawed in half, and others were killed with the sword. …. God had something better in mind for us, so that they would not reach perfection without us." Rev. Owens knows that his quest for freedom is helping to complete the lives of those who have gone before us. He believes increasing freedom for black Americans will increase freedom for all Americans and will honor those who have given their lives for our freedom.

In this seasoned time in his life, Rev. Owens fears not to speak the truth. He has had death threats and has been called the n-word by many left-wingers — along with many other evil and racist names. Rev. Owens boldly speaks the truth. In the early 1990s, during the unraveling of the old Soviet Union, many die-hard Communists and Russian citizens refused to believe the truth. They told themselves that everything was all right because they had witnessed the demonstration of power as the Soviet army with all its glorious weapons paraded down the streets in front of the Kremlin. But the system was failing and soon collapsed. In many aspects, the American socialist-leftist agenda today can be compared to the decaying communist rule in the old Soviet Union. Look at all the hopelessness in major American inner cities today where Democrat-socialist politicians run the majority of these heavily populated metro complexes. Rev. Owens explains in this book why black Americans must vote their Christian values if they ever want to, "cross the Jordan River."

Dr. Martin Luther King has been compared to Moses because he led black America out of the bondage of segregation. Will black Americans ever make it to the Promised Land? After reading this book and acting on what it says, one day, we may say that Rev. Owens' dream was like Joshua leading all Americans into the Promised Land of prosperity for all!

Dr. Edd Holliday, Tupelo, MS

Rev. Bill Owens has worked hard to bring about political and social change. He detests discrimination based on color, religion, sex, or national origin. He is passionate about educating the African American people by remaining biblical focused and sound. One of his most significant accomplishments is his compelling book, "A Dream Derailed," which provides insight as he guides us on a detailed journey. Rev.Bill Owens, his loving and devoted wife Deborah and their beautiful children are valuable friends to my wife and me.I now have the privilege of pastoring them at The Faith International Church of God in Christ in Houston, Texas. Our relationship has withstood the test of time and distance.

Bishop Charles E. Brown I, Prelate of Greater New Orleans Jurisdiction of Louisiana; Vice President, Coalition of African American Pastors

Our Sponsors

Kenneth Adamek

Jodell Allinger

Charles Anceney

Kevin Anderson

Jennifer Arroyo

Herman Baker

J.C.& Jill Basnight

William Berggren

David Bliss

Robert Borchardt

Peter Bos

Layne Boyer

Dale Boylston

Arnold Brevick

Holly Bridwell

Bishop Charles and First Lady Brown

Jeff Brown

Robinson Brown

Mary Bruce

Ray Bruno

Sheila Campbell

Tammy Canon

Hong Chen

Steve & Tammy Cleary

Dr. Grady Core

Michael Cronin

Joseph Daltorio

Johnny Deal
Jeannine Der Manouel
Americo DiLoretto
Robert Dorantes
Richard Eaton
Laura Edge
Michael & Deborah Edwards
David Embry
Mark & Kellyanne Engel
Robin Exner
Thomas Fame
William Flow
Pastor and Mrs. Tom Ford
Daniel Frettinger
Charles Gill
Stephen Goostree
John Greiner
Jeffrey Harvey
Brian Hatch
James B Heisler
Patricia Hershwitzky
Catherine Hirsch
Clyde Holley
Dr. Ed and Leslie Holliday
Dr. Steven and Janie Hotze
Mary Howald
Craig Hudak
Timothy Hunt
Jeffrey Jacobson
Daria James
Alysa Jarvis
Calvin Jones

Elza Jones
Phillip Kelly
Naullain Kendrick
Evangelist Alveda King
Sheila Kuenzle
Leah Langlois
Marian Liles
Cheryl Livingston
Susan Madole
Eddy Martin
Paolo Masetti
Greg McAfee
J Thomas McCalman
Robin McCauley
John Meadows
Jo-Ann Lemon Miller
Jennifer Montoya
John Moore
Jeffrey Morgan
David Murdock
John Nowak
Renee Peters
Cynthia Pettigrew
Cynthia Pflumm
Benjamin Phillips
Greg Pond
David Poss
Vicki Ratliff
Juanita Rathfon
Michael Reavey
Liz Reed
Spencer Reed

Lisa Remmer
Cathy Richter
James and Leslie Rigney
Eric Roberts
James Sarafin
Ruth Ann Saxon
Ralph and Linda Schmidt
James Sharp
Sydney Sheridan
Joyce Slingerland
Dave Smith
Phil and Mary Smith
Rowland Snowdon
Mark Sommerfield
Jennifer Spooner
Laura Tillmon
Joseph Todd
Sally Todd
Laura Toelle
Allen Trimble
Albert VanPelt
Linda Vega
Leanne Wade
Rev. David Welch
Gerald Whitmarsh
Jim Wilder
Georgina Winslow
Chris Wood
Pamela Zieburtz

References

1. King, Martin L., Jr. "I Have a Dream." Lincoln Memorial, Washington, D.C. 28 Aug. 1963. *American Rhetoric*, 25 Mar. 2013, http://www.americanrhetoric.com/speeches/mlkihave adream.htm. Accessed 2 July 2019.

2. King, Martin L., Jr. "Letter from a Birmingham Jail." 16 April 1963, *The Martin Luther King, Jr. Research and Education Institute*, https://kinginstitute.stanford.edu/king-papers/-documents/letter-birmingham-jail. Accessed 2 July 2019.

3. "Slavery and the Abolition Society." *Benjamin Franklin Historical Society*, http://www.benjamin-franklin-history.org/slavery-abolition-society/. Accessed 2 July 2019.

4. "Citizen Ben: Abolitionist." *PBS*, http://www.pbs.org/-benfranklin/l3_citizen_abolitionist.html. Accessed 2 July 2019.

5. "Slavery and the Making of America: The Slave Experience." *PBS*, https://www.thirteen.org/wnet/-slavery/experience/freedom/docs13.html. Accessed 2 July 2019.

6. Federer, William. "American Minute: John Quincy Adams." *Fairfax Free Citizen*. https://fairfaxfreecitizen.com/2018/02/21/american-minute-177/.

7. Federer, William. "American Minute: Politics of Race." *American Minute*, http://archive.constantcontact.com/-fs155/1108762609255/archive/1121775118075.html. Accessed 2 July 2019.

8. H.R. 7152, Civil Rights Act of 1964. "House Vote #182 in 1964." *GovTrack*, https://www.govtrack.us/congress/votes/88-1964/h182. Accessed July 2019

9. HR. 7152, Civil Rights Act of 1964. "Senate Vote #409 in 1964." *GovTrack*, https://www.govtrack.us/congress/votes/88-1964/s409. Accessed 2 July 2019.

10. Kessler, Ronald. *Inside the White House: The Hidden Lives of the Modern Presidents and the Secrets of the World's Most Powerful Institution*. New York, NY: Pocket Books. 2 Aug. 1995.

11. Caro, Robert A. *Master of the Senate: The Years of Lyndon Johnson*. New York: Knopf. 2002.

12. Serwer, Adam. "Lyndon Johnson was a civil rights hero. But also a racist." *MSNBC*, 12 April 2014, http://www.msnbc.com/msnbc/lyndon-johnson-civil-rights-racism. Accessed 2 July 2019.

13. Parker, Robert. *Capitol Hill in Black and White*. Jove,1989.

14. Dallek, Robert. *Flawed Giant: Lyndon Johnson and His Times, 1961-1973*. New York: Oxford University Press, 1998.

15. Democratic Platform Committee. "The 2016 Democratic Platform." *Democrats*, https://democrats.org/about/party-platform/. Accessed 2 July 2019.

16. 2016 Republican National Convention. *Republican Platform 2016*. https://prod-static-ngop-pbl.s3.amazonaws.com/-media/documents/DRAFT_12_FINAL[1]-ben_1468872234.pdf. Accessed 2 July 2019.

17. *Coalition of African-American Pastors*. https://caapusa.org/. Accessed 2 July 2019.

18. *Education for All*. http://www.missioneducation.org/. Accessed 2 July 2019.

19. National Assessment of Educational Progress. "2017 NAEP Mathematics and Reading Assessments." National Center for Education Statistics. *The Nation's Report Card*, https://www.nationsreportcard.gov/reading_math_201 7_highlights/. Accessed 2 July 2019.

20. Balingit, Moriah. "U.S. schoolchildren tumble in international reading exam rankings, worrying educators." *The Washington Post*, 5 Dec. 2017, https://www.washingtonpost.com/news/education/wp/2 017/12/05/u-s-schoolchildren-tumble-in-international-reading-exam-rankings-worrying-educators/?utm_term=.911d6b5c58bb. Accessed 2 July 2019.

21. United States Department of Education, National Commission on Excellence in Education. *A Nation at Risk: the Imperative for Educational Reform: a Report to the Nation and the Secretary of Education.* Washington, DC: The Commission : [Supt. of Docs., U.S. G.P.O. distributor], 1983. https://www2.ed.gov/pubs/NatAtRisk/risk.html. Accessed 2 July 2019.

22. Bureau of Labor Statistics. "Employment Situation Summary." *United States Department of Labor*, April 2018, https://www.bls.gov/news.release/empsit.nr0.htm. Accessed 2 July 2019.

23. Owens, William. "Abandon the Democratic Party." *The Washington Times*. 26 Oct. 2016. Page A3. https://caapusa.org/2016/10/read-caaps-open-letter/

24. Goldberg, Jonah. *Liberal Fascism: The Secret History of the American Left, from Mussolini to the Politics of Change.* New York: Broadway Books, 2007.

25. Jackson, Jr., Harry. "Food Stamps: Policy or Political Payoff." *Townhall*, 25 Feb. 2013, https://townhall.com/columnists/harryrjacksonjr/2013/

02/25/food-stamps-policy-or-political-payoff-n1519830. Accessed 2 July 2019.

26. Saslow, Eli. "In Florida, a food-stamp recruiter deals with wrenching choices." *The Washington Post*, 23 April 2013, https://www.washingtonpost.com/national/in-florida-a-food-stamp-recruiter-deals-with-wrenching-choices/2013/04/23/b3d6b41c-a3a4-11e2-9c03-6952ff305f35_story.html?utm_term=.0b94e427e793. Accessed 2 July 2019.

27. Sheffield, Rachel. "Uncle Sam Wants You…on Food Stamps?" *The Daily Signal*, 30 April 2013, https://www.dailysignal.com/2013/04/30/uncle-sam-wants-you-on-food-stamps/. Accessed 2 July 2019.

28. United States Department of Agriculture. "Supplemental Nutrition Assistance Program Participation and Costs (Data as of March 8, 2019)." https://fns-prod.azureedge.net/sites/-default/files/pd/SNAPsummary.pdf. Accessed 2 July 2019.

29. Sheffield, Rachel. "Big bank account? No problem. You may still qualify for food stamps." *The Daily Signal*, 27 Jan., 2014, https://www.dailysignal.com/2014/01/27/big-bank-account-problem-may-still-qualify-food-stamps/. Accessed 2 July 2019.

30. Dewey, Caitlin. Republican plan to tighten food stamp work requirements advances despite opposition. *The Washington Post*, 18 April 2018, https://www.washingtonpost.com/news/wonk/wp/2018/04/18/the-republican-plan-to-tighten-food-stamp-work-requirements-is-advancing-without-a-single-democrats-vote/?noredirect=on&utm_term=.3ea35e86634b. Accessed 2 July 2019.

31. "Abortion and African Americans." *Life Dynamics*, https://lifedynamics.com/busted-the-abortion-industry/abortion-african-americans/. 2 July 2019.

32. Chapman, Michael. "NYC: More black babies killed by abortion than born." *CNSNews*, 20 Feb. 2014, https://www.cnsnews.com/news/article/michael-w-chapman/nyc-more-black-babies-killed-abortion-born. Accessed 2 July 2019.

33. Jatlaoui Tara, et al. Abortion Surveillance — United States, 2014. MMWR *Surveill Summaries* 2017;66(No. SS-24):1–48. DOI: http://dx.doi.org/10.15585/mmwr.ss6624a1. Accessed 2 July 2019.

34. "Abortion and race: for decades, abortion has disproportionately eliminated minority babies." *Abort73.com*, http://abort73.com/abortion/abortion_and_race/. Accessed 2 July 2019.

35. Sanger, Margaret. *The Pivot of Civilization*. New York: Brentano's Publishers, 1922.

36. The Margaret Sanger Papers Project. "Birth control or race control? Sanger and the Negro Project." *New York University*, 2001, https://www.nyu.edu/projects/sanger/articles/-bc_or_race_control.php. Accessed 2 July 2019.

37. "The Foundation that Just Gave Planned Parenthood an Award Also Funded its Eugenics Projects." *Saynsumthn's Blog*, https://saynsumthn.wordpress.com/tag/mary-and-lasker-foundation/. Accessed 2 July 2019.

38. Vance, Kevin. "Secretary Clinton stands by her praise of eugenicist Margaret Sanger." *The Weekly Standard*, 15 April 2009, https://www.weeklystandard.com/kevin-vance/sec-clinton-stands-by-her-praise-of-eugenicist-margaret-sanger. Accessed 2 July 2019.

39. Planned Parenthood. "2016-2017 Annual Report." *Planned Parenthood*, https://www.plannedparenthood.org/uploads/-filer_public/d4/50/d450c016-a6a9-4455-bf7f-

711067db5ff7/20171229_ar16-17_p01_lowres.pdf.
Accessed 2 July 2019.

40. Studnicki, James and Fisher, John. Planned
Parenthood: Supply Induced Demand for Abortion in
the US. *Open Journal of Preventive Medicine*. 2018.
8, 142-145. doi: 10.4236/ojpm.2018.84014.

41. Donovan, Charles and Studnicki, James. "Planned
Parenthood: 'Irreplaceable' and 'Lifesaving'?"
Charlotte Lozier Institute, 2017,
https://lozierinstitute.org/planned-parenthood--
irreplaceable-and-lifesaving/. Accessed 2 July 2019.

42. "Rise." *Coalition of African-American Pastors,*
http://caapusa.org/membership/rise/. Accessed 2 July
2019.

43. King, Martin Luther, Jr. "Rediscovering Lost Values."
*Stanford University: The Martin Luther King, Jr. Papers
Project*, 28 Feb. 1954,
https://swap.stanford.edu/20141218223358/http://mlk
-
kpp01.stanford.edu/primarydocuments/Vol2/540228R
ediscoveringLostValues.pdf. Accessed 2 July 2019.

44. Harrison, J.D. "The decline of American
entrepreneurship –
in five charts." *The Washington Post*, 12 Feb. 2015,
https://www.washingtonpost.com/news/on-small-
business/wp/2015/02/12/the-decline-of-american-
entrepreneurship-in-five-
charts/?noredirect=on&utm_term=.f7f69a8236d2.
Accessed 2 July 2019.

SPECIAL REPORT
YALE UNIVERSITY

Do Early Educators' Implicit Biases Regarding Sex and Race Relate to Behavior Expectations and Recommendations of Preschool Expulsions and Suspensions?

- In a research study examining race and sex bias in preschool, researchers at the Yale Child Study Center found that teachers tended to more closely watch blacks than whites (especially black boys) when "challenging behaviors are expected."
- Using eye-tracking technology, researchers measured how much time teachers spent looking at students of different races and sexes when told to look for possible behavioral problems. Both white and black teachers spent more time looking at the black boy than the other children. (All of the children were exhibiting normal behavior.)
- When asked, 42 percent of the teachers said the black boy required the most attention, followed by the white boy at 34 percent.
- Black teachers appeared to hold black students to a higher standard, as black teachers spent the most time watching the black boy for behavioral problems. The researchers stated that this could reflect, "a belief that black children require harsh assessment and discipline to prepare them for a harsh world."
- Black teachers tended to rate the behavior of black boys more severely (in the absence of any background information) and were

more likely to recommend exclusionary discipline (e.g., suspension or expulsion).

- The teachers', vignettes describing problematic behavior in a preschool student, such as acting out, pushing classmates, and ignoring the teacher. The fictional student was then given different names differentiating race and sex (i.e. Jake, Latoya, Emily, and DeShawn). Black teachers were more demanding of black students than white teachers. Moreover, black teachers were more likely to recommend exclusionary discipline in general.

- When the students in the vignettes were given a backstory involving a difficult home life (including a violent father and a mother working multiple jobs), the teachers showed more empathy - but only to students of the same race. When the child and teacher were of different races, the teacher was more likely to rate the behavior as harder to fix and more severely problematic

- Researchers speculated that the more lenient attitude of white teachers toward black boys could reflect a stereotype that black students are more likely to misbehave.

- "The tendency to base classroom observation on the gender and race of the child may explain in part why those children are more frequently identified as misbehaving and hence why there is a racial disparity in the discipline." -- Walter S. Gilliam, director of The Edward Zigler Center in Child Development and Social Policy (and one of the researchers who conducted the study)

Source:
Gilliam, Walter S., et al. "Do Early Educators' Implicit Biases Regarding Sex and Race Relate to Behavior Expectations and Recommendations of Preschool Expulsions and Suspensions?" Yale University Child Study Center, 28 Sept. 2016
https://medicine.yale.edu/childstudy/zigler/publications/Preschool%20Implicit%20Bias%20Policy%20Brief_final_9_26_276766_5379_v1.pdf. Accessed 28 Sept. 2019.

Download the entire report:

Did you Know?

1. Americans pay billions to large corporations to not hire U.S. citizens?
2. Nearly three-quarters of Silicon Valley workers are foreign-born.
3. American cities with the largest homeless populations are all Democrat-run enclaves.
4. Illegal immigration may have cost Black Americans more than 1 million jobs.
5. Christianity is the world's most persecuted religion.

NOTES

_____

_____

_____

_____

_____

_____

_____

_____

_____

_____

NOTES

Connect with Us:

www.caapusa.org / **info@caapusa.org**